101
FASCINATING
Golf
FACTS

101 Fascinating Facts Series

DAVID McPHERSON

101 FASCINATING Golf FACTS

DUNDURN
PRESS

Publisher: Meghan Macdonald | Acquiring editor: Kathryn Lane | Editor: Dominic Farrell
Cover designer: Karen Alexiou
Cover image: golf clubs: Incomible/shutterstock.com; ball: FeelplusCreator/shutterstock.com; background: designed by Freepik

Library and Archives Canada Cataloguing in Publication

Title: 101 fascinating golf facts / David McPherson.
Other titles: One hundred one fascinating golf facts
Names: McPherson, David (Music journalist), author
Description: Series statement: 101 fascinating facts ; 4
Identifiers: Canadiana (print) 20240484495 | Canadiana (ebook) 20240484509 | ISBN 9781459754287 (softcover) | ISBN 9781459754294 (PDF) | ISBN 9781459754300 (EPUB)
Subjects: LCSH: Gold—Miscellanea. | LCSH: Gold—Canada—Miscellanea. | LCGFT: Trivia and miscellanea.
Classification: LCC GV967 .M47 2025 | DDC 796.35202—dc23

We acknowledge the support of the Canada Council for the Arts and the Ontario Arts Council for our publishing program. We also acknowledge the financial support of the Government of Ontario, through the Ontario Book Publishing Tax Credit and Ontario Creates, and the Government of Canada.

Care has been taken to trace the ownership of copyright material used in this book. The author and the publisher welcome any information enabling them to rectify any references or credits in subsequent editions.

The publisher is not responsible for websites or their content unless they are owned by the publisher.

Printed and bound in Canada.

Dundurn Press
1382 Queen Street East
Toronto, Ontario, Canada M4L 1C9
dundurn.com, @dundurnpress

To Rube for encouraging a young scribe
to follow his golf writing dreams.

INTRODUCTION

I'll never forget Christmas morning in 1984. After opening our stockings to see what Santa had brought, my dad turned to my mom, sister, and me and told us there was one final gift to open. Hidden among the branches on my grandparents' artificial tree lay a white envelope. Inside was a handwritten note from my father letting us know that we were all now members of Westmount Golf & Country Club. Starting that spring, this private club in Kitchener, perennially ranked as one of the top twenty courses in Canada, became my home away from home. We were fortunate to live on a crescent adjacent to the eighth hole. This is where I learned to love this great game. I'm forever grateful to my dad for this present.

Writing, like golf, is a cherished part of my life. It was natural as I progressed in my writing career to seek subjects

I was interested in. I thank bestselling author and longtime *Globe and Mail* golf columnist Lorne Rubenstein for encouraging my writing about the game and championing my work. He met this aspiring golf scribe, at the time a stranger, for a coffee to share some of his insights and experiences. In the ensuing years, we've become friends and enjoyed many golf games together.

My first published magazine story appeared in *Golf Canada* in 1999. Since then, my byline has appeared in numerous publications, from SCOREGolf to *Golf Digest*. I covered a pair of Canadian Opens for PGATOUR.com, have attended the Masters, and have been fortunate to play courses where the pros play from Washington State to Colombia. I have also had the honour of serving a two-year term as the president of the Golf Journalists Association of Canada. Golf has not only allowed me to travel and enjoy many bucket-list experiences, but the game has also been a conduit for me to meet many friends along the way.

I've written about all aspects of the game — from the players, both professional and amateur, to the courses, the architecture, and the maintenance of these fields where friendships are formed, memories are made, and dreams are realized. I've tried to capture this passion in the 101 fascinating stories in this collection. I hope you enjoy reading them as much as I enjoyed writing them.

THE BREAKFAST BALL

Origin stories often generate debate, especially when they rely on oral rather than written history. Not surprisingly, the origin of the term "mulligan" — a noun referring to a do-over in golf — and how it came into the golf lexicon is contested. In *The Historical Dictionary of Golfing Terms: From 1500 to the Present*, Peter Davies wrote "origin obscure" in the term's definition. Despite competing histories of the word's beginnings, the majority of golf historians stand by one that stars a Canadian.

According to the United States Golf Association, the word is attributed to Montreal native David Mulligan. During the 1920s, the hotelier, who was part owner of the Biltmore Hotel in New York City, played at the Country Club of Montreal. While it's widely accepted that the freebie is named after the man, the story of how, when, or why this term was coined is a little less certain.

There are three versions. In the first, he made an impulsive decision to retake his opening shot after hitting a lengthy drive that was far from straight. The businessman told his playing partners that this was a "correction shot." The second version claims Mr. Mulligan took a do-over because he had to drive over a bumpy road to arrive at his home course. As a result, by the time he stood ready to hit on the first tee he was more nervous than a teenager before their driver's exam — and so he took a second tee shot after his nerves settled. The third version of the story is similar. Since the hotelier was frequently late for his tee time, he was often flustered and rushed when he arrived. So, a mulligan became routine. This first do-over — or breakfast ball as it is also called today because these shots are often taken early in the morning when a golfer has no time to warm up — caught on when Mulligan moved to the United States and shared this unofficial rule with other golfers.

Others argue that John A. Mulligan, a locker room attendant at Essex Fells Country Club in New Jersey, deserves credit for the word's origin. When Mulligan, affectionately known as Buddy, was not cleaning members' shoes or doing the laundry, he often joined members for a round. One day, Buddy asked his playing partners for a do-over since he did not get to warm up or practise like they could. Word got around about Buddy's second-chance shot, and other players started to adopt the practice. Apparently, one of his playing partners was an editor for the local newspaper and started to include the term "mulligan" in print when describing this practice.

No matter who the word is named in honour of — or what the true origin of the term is — mulligans are not sanctioned in the official rules of golf. If you want to take one, golf etiquette requires that you always make sure your playing partners agree. The accepted practice allows for just one mulligan per round. I thank whichever Mulligan coined this term as I, and no doubt many readers, have used this second-chance shot countless times while enjoying a recreational round, when the experience is more important than the score.

GOLF ON THE MOON

The most remote place a golf ball has been struck is found not on Earth but in outer space. On February 6, 1971, Alan Shepard, the first American to travel to space a decade before, became the first person to golf on the moon. With one mighty swing — well … it was more like a one-handed shank — Shepard made history again.

Shepard was the commander of the Apollo 14 lunar mission. NASA was unaware of — and did not sanction — the forty-seven-year-old's plans to hit a golf ball on the lunar surface. The veteran astronaut, who was an avid golfer, came up with the idea and kept it secret. He had the pro from Oaks Country Club in Texas (Jack Harden) build him a modified head for a Wilson Staff Dynapower 6-iron, which he then hid in his space suit along with a few golf balls in his socks. The rumour is that the mission director was the only person who knew of Shepard's plan; he went along with the astronaut on the promise that the golf shot would happen only if there was time after all parts of the mission were successfully completed.

After nine hours of exploring the lunar surface, the chance arrived. With the world watching (NASA broadcast the Apollo 14 moon landing live in colour), Shepard revealed his homemade club, which he had attached to a tool designed for scooping lunar rock samples, turned to the TV cameras, and said: "Houston … you might recognize what I have in my hand as the handle for the contingency sample return. It just so happens to have a genuine six iron on the bottom of it. In my left hand, I have a little white pellet that's familiar to millions of Americans…. Unfortunately, the suit is so stiff, I can't do this with two hands, but I'm going to try a little sand-trap shot here."

Shepard swung four times. The first two were whiffs, and he hit mainly moon dust. The third shot he shanked into a nearby crater, causing capsule communicator Fred Haise in the Houston command room to joke, "That looked like a slice to me, Al!" Finally, on the fourth try, Shepard made better contact and exclaimed to the millions glued to their TV sets on earth, with a little hyperbole of course, "Miles and miles and miles!"

The reality is no one measured Shepard's moon shot, so it was hard to guess how far it really travelled. Decades later, an English photography hobbyist, Andy Saunders, after digitally enhancing the still photos from all the Apollo missions (including this one), was able to calculate the distance. By studying the images, he figured out, by superimposing images from that historic February day with footage from the Lunar Reconnaissance Orbiter satellite captured in 2009, that Shepard's shot had actually only travelled forty yards.

No matter how far that ball flew, in the end Shepard took the game of golf farther than it had ever been.

3
GOLF ABOVE THE CLOUDS

Adventure travellers, pack your clubs for a pair of courses that, while not for the faint of heart, are definitely bucket-list worthy. Just be sure to include extra oxygen and some Diamox to ward off acute mountain sickness.

The first stop on this high-altitude sporting expedition is the Yak Golf Course and Environmental Park in India. Named after the long-haired, oxlike animal that roams these mountain peaks, the eighteen holes sit at 3,800 metres above sea level in Kupup, East Sikkim. First established in 1972, the course is managed by the Indian Army, since it is located within one of its bases; this makes securing a tee time challenging, but not impossible. Foreigners require a special permit to enter the park.

Surrounded by the Himalayas, the course is open for play seven days a week from May to December. Periodic closures are common due to high winds and other weather-related events. From January to April, the environmental park turns into a winter sports destination for skiing, ice skating, and hockey. No golf carts are allowed at the Yak, but if you need help carrying your clubs, those long-haired beasts the course is named after will lug them for you.

Until 2022, the Yak held the Guinness World Record for the world's highest golf course. Now, a new nine-hole track in Nepal — Mustang Golf Course — has taken the honour. At 4,600 metres above sea level, the course eclipses the Yak by eight hundred metres. Only about a thousand of the thirty-one million people living in Nepal are golfers, but the country boasts a professional tour and seven courses.

The nine-hole Mustang Golf Course was built on a sliver of land previously used for grazing horses. Located above Lo Manthang, the capital of the Upper Mustang region of Nepal, the course sits on an ancient trade route between Nepal and Tibet. Local politician Indra Dhara Bista was inspired after a visit to the United States. After seeing courses built in Arizona's deserts, he sold the idea to his constituents as a way to boost tourism.

The cost for building the golf course was one million Nepali rupees (about $7,840), which was drawn from the Constituency Infrastructure Development Fund. There are plans to build an additional nine holes in the future. To spur tourism and promote this new wonder, the first Top of the World Golf Classic, with twenty-eight competitors, was held in the course's inaugural year. The second annual event, held in September 2023, saw forty competitors register, and a horse was offered as a prize if anyone aced the par 3 sixth hole!

Golfers are required to pay $500 to obtain a restricted-area trekking permit to access the Upper Mustang where the course is located. Before setting out on this golf journey above the clouds, drinking some hot tea is recommended to build strength.

The trip is definitely worth it: the vistas of the surrounding mountain ranges are jaw-dropping. Playing the course has its challenges — landslides are a way of life, especially during monsoon season, so there is always a chance that your tee time is changed. But, hey, golf at high altitude is a bucket-list item for a reason and demands patience. Just sip a Nepalese tea and wait it out.

LIFESTYLES OF THE GOLF RICH AND FAMOUS

Golf is an expensive sport — the equipment re- quired and the green fees to participate can set you back quite a bit. How expensive can it get? If you really want to splurge, there is no shortage of clubs where, for most of us, the entry fee is prohibitively expensive. And it's not surprising to learn that it's in Las Vegas, where everything is marketed as bigger and better, you can find the most expensive public course.

Shadow Creek Golf Course opened in 1989 and cost $60 million to build. The course, designed by American architect Tom Fazio, was initially ultra-private; tee times were only available to owner Steve Wynn and his buddies. In 2000 MGM Resorts International took over ownership and offered tee times for $500. Today, that green fee is more than $1,250 in peak season. The club does include an incentive: if you are a registered guest of one of the company's Las Vegas resorts, a limo drive to and from the course, services of a caddie (tip extra), and a locker for the day are all included with the green fee.

If four figures for this Sin City experience is out of your budget, for a mere $900 you can enjoy the challenge of the famous island green at the Players Stadium Course at TPC Sawgrass (home of the PGA Tour's Players Championship).

If you're looking for a playground right out of an episode of *Lifestyles of the Rich and Famous* rather than a daily-fee course, the Madison Club is where you want to go. It is the world's most expensive private club to join. Just to get in the door of this gated golf community in La Quinta, California, will require payment of a $500,000 initiation fee. Like the majority of private clubs, annual fees are not listed, but sources estimate they run you another $70,000. But, hey, for that, you get to hobnob with members such as Apple CEO Tim Cook and the Kardashians.

Amenities beyond the golf course include a private movie theatre, full-service spa, fitness facility, game lounge, an eighteen-hole putting course, and miles of hiking and horseback-riding trails. You'll never go hungry during your round as the Madison features what the club dubs "discovery comfort stations" all along the course where members and guests can enjoy treats like ice-cream sandwiches and tacos. For $500,000, those tacos should include Wagyu beef!

"I'LL CARRY FOR YOU," SISTER

There's nothing so beautiful as sisterly love.
Canadian golf siblings Brooke and Brittany Henderson
epitomize this bond, sharing their passion each week as they
work together as a team on the Ladies Professional Golf
Association (LPGA) Tour.

Brittany, a former Quebec junior champion and U.S.
college player, and one-time member of the developmental
professional tour — the junior tour below the LPGA —
gave up her golf dreams in 2014 shortly after her little sister,
at just seventeen years old, won her first ever event — the
Portland Classic. Brittany has now been on the bag for
all but one of the thirteen LPGA tournaments, which include a pair of major championships, that Brooke has won.
Already, Brooke has won more tournaments than any other

Canadian professional golfer (man or woman) in the history of the LPGA and PGA Tours. Trophies include two majors: the 2016 Women's PGA Championship and the 2022 Evian Championship. She is also a three-time Olympian (2016, 2020, 2024).

This sisterly sacrifice — and the special bond between these golf siblings — inspired Songwriters Hall of Fame member Chip Taylor (born James Voight) to pen an ode to the Hendersons. This love reminded him of the relationship he shares with his brother, actor Jon Voight. Taylor, best known for "Wild Thing" — the song the Troggs took to number one in 1966 — has also had his compositions covered by everyone from Janis Joplin and Aretha Franklin to Dusty Springfield and Frank Sinatra.

Outside of music, the songwriter has always loved golf; his father was a golf professional, and during his formative years, Chip competed in many amateur tournaments. Before his success as a singer-songwriter, he worked briefly as a golf pro. His stage name (Chip) derives from his precision around the greens.

When not touring or writing, one of Taylor's favourite pastimes is watching golf, especially the LPGA Tour. After watching Brooke play and learning more about the captivating story of the bond between her and her sister, the songwriter immortalized the Hendersons' heartwarming tale in his 2016 song "I'll Carry for You."

NOT SO TRIVIAL A PURSUIT AT THE PULPIT CLUB

Category: Sports & Leisure
Question: Name the golf property opened by a pair of ex-newspapermen from Canada who created what *Time* magazine called "the biggest phenomenon in game history."
Answer: The Pulpit Club.

•

On a mid-December afternoon in 1979, Chris Haney, a highschool dropout who became the youngest photo editor in Canadian Press (CP) history before moving on to the *Montreal Gazette*, and Scott Abbott, a CP sports editor, paused their Scrabble game after discovering a tile was missing. This break turned into a brainstorming session in which the two friends ruminated on how to create a pastime just as popular as this word-making game.

The Trivial Pursuit concept came quickly. But moving from idea to implementation took some time. The pair spent hundreds of hours writing questions, and they had to solicit seed money from friends and family willing to take a risk on the game's success. In 1981 the board game was commercially released. Sales were sluggish the first couple of years. But by 1983, word of mouth and a big marketing push in the United States made Trivial Pursuit the game everyone wanted. Annual sales regularly were in the millions, and within a few years, it had become the biggest-selling board game in Canadian history. Parker Brothers bought the licensing rights in 1988. And in 2008, Hasbro bought all the rights for a cool $80 million. Long before this sale, the royalties from global sales allowed Haney, Abbott, and their initial thirty-two investors (who shelled out $1,000 each) to not worry about money.

What did these two ex-newspapermen do with these newfound riches? Beyond building palatial estates, buying racehorses, and living a life of luxury, the pair created Devil's Pulpit in 1990. The story is that the two often enjoyed a game of golf, and, one day when they could not secure a tee time, they decided to build their own course. American architects Michael Hurdzan and Dana Fry designed the eighteen-hole course, which is located north of Toronto in the rolling hills of Caledon. The name derives from a rock formation visible on the property when you stand on the seventh tee. *Golf Magazine* awarded Devil's Pulpit the Best New Course in Canada prize when it opened, and it has been ranked one of the top one hundred in the country ever since. A second course, the Paintbrush, was constructed on the property a couple of years later.

Lorne Rubenstein, the dean of Canadian golf writers, has said of this special place, "Members are very fortunate to belong to the best two-course club in the world." This is no hyperbole. From the elevated first tee, one glimpses Toronto's skyline. That silhouette of the CN Tower is the only indication a big city is near. Once your game begins, you become lost in the beauty of the landscape on this challenging and very distinct pair of courses. The Pulpit offers a parkland experience while the Paintbrush provides a links experience, complete with grazing sheep.

Here's the baaaa-ckstory on that: Ken Wright, the property's original superintendent, and his assistant, Jayson Griffiths, who is now the director of agronomy and grounds at the London Hunt Club, always thought that grazing sheep would be a great fit at the Paintbrush, helping to make it feel even more like a traditional Scottish links course. This wish came true in 2020 when fifteen Suffolk black-faced sheep were brought onto the property. While the original reason the club added the sheep was to enhance the links feel, they offer the added benefit of helping to reduce labour, since these animals naturally keep the fescue under control, saving staff from cutting it back each fall.

Unfortunately, Haney died young, in 2010, following kidney and circulatory problems at just fifty-nine years old. But what a legacy he leaves: Along with a game that has sold more than one hundred million copies globally, these two golf courses, known today as the Pulpit Club, created because he and Abbott could not get a tee time, remain a living monument and two of the finest courses in Canada.

WHO NEEDS FOURTEEN CLUBS?

Rule 4 from the *Rules of Golf* states players are "limited to no more than fourteen clubs." The United States Golf Association and the R&A (the governing golf body for the United Kingdom) both adopted this rule in 1936 as a way to curtail the ridiculous number of clubs some professionals were carrying. In the days of hickory-shafted sticks, players usually carried between six and ten clubs, but with the broad acceptance of steel-shafted clubs in the late 1920s, the number of clubs that players carried began to rise dramatically. During this transitional period, as players adjusted to these new pieces of equipment, they wanted to still have the hickory sticks at their disposal. Lawson Little, who won the 1940 U.S. Open, is one of the main reasons the governing bodies changed the rules to a fourteen-club limit. Before Little turned pro, when he won the 1934 and 1935 British and U.S. Amateurs, he carried as many as thirty clubs in his bag, including seven wedges!

On the other side of the spectrum, American Chick Evans proved more is not necessarily better when he won the "Double Crown" — the U.S. Open and the U.S. Amateur — in 1916 using only seven clubs. In modern golf, there is a club to suit most any situation a player faces on the course. There are hybrids that bridge the loft gap between woods and irons and wedges with lofts of fifty-eight degrees or more, specifically designed to lob the ball high in the air. The choice of which of those fourteen clubs most golfers carry to use is almost endless.

Boredom can often lead to creativity. An Arizona golfer supported this theory in 2020 when he made national headlines for winning a golf tournament using only a putter. What possessed Anthony Griggs to try such a stunt? Initially, he was simply seeking a new challenge; he loved the game but he was becoming somewhat frustrated by the sameness of the matches he was playing. That Wilson putter he bought for $2.99 at his local Goodwill has now won him nine tournaments. Can you imagine hitting a golf ball with a putter an average of 225 yards — more than the average distance a player hits a tee shot with a driver? Well, that is what Griggs can do.

What is the Guinness World Record for the lowest score using just one club? That belongs to American Thad Daber, who shot a two-under par 70 using only a 6-iron at the 1987 World One Club Championship at Lochmere Golf Club in Cary, North Carolina.

WHAT ARE THE ODDS?

Most golfers play the sport their entire lives with- out getting this holy grail. We're talking about a hole-in-one. For most amateurs, the odds of scoring what is also called an ace are 12,500 to 1 — not much better than the chances of getting hit by lightning (1 in 15,300)! And even the odds for professionals are pretty steep: 2,500 to 1.

To get a hole-in-one requires skill and usually a little luck: the right bounce at the right time, or maybe help from Mother Nature on a windy day.

Thomas Mitchell Morris, better known as Old Tom Morris, made one of the first aces ever recorded in 1868 at the Open Championship at Prestwick. Tiger Woods made his first when he was just six. A few other fascinating facts about holes-in-one to ponder next time you finish playing without getting one and are a wee discouraged:

- Only 1 to 2 percent of golfers score an ace in a year.
- On average, a golfer will have to play twenty-four years before making an ace.
- The Guinness World Record for youngest golfer to ever make a hole-in-one is American Christian Carpenter. He was four years and 195 days old when made the ace on December 18, 1999, at Mountain View Golf Club in Hickory, North Carolina.
- Mancil Davis, the self-proclaimed King of the Aces, holds the world record for greatest number of holes-in-one: fifty-one.
- Golfers scoring an ace usually have to buy a drink for everyone on the course when they accomplish the feat. It's unclear when this tradition started, but there are newspaper stories referring to what's called hole-in-one insurance as early as 1918. It's ironic that for this odds-defying shot the golfer who accomplishes the feat is not the one rewarded.
- A hole-in-one on a par 5 is called a condor, and the number of these recorded in the game's history can be counted on one hand.

LINGO ON THE LINKS

One wonders if the first golfers were also avid ornithologists. That is an easy assumption to make when you learn the names for what various under-par scores are called: birdie, eagle, albatross, and condor. However, investigation into the origin of these golf terms reveals that the many avian terms in golf are not the legacy of bird lovers. Rather, because birdie was the first under-par score coined, later terms simply followed suit with specific scores named after different species of bird.

The word "birdie," a score of one under par on a hole, derives from an early twentieth-century American slang term meaning "excellent." The word initially referred to any stupendous hit, for which you complimented your playing partner by saying, "That was a bird of a shot!" "Birdie" was first used on a golf course at the Atlantic City Country Club, when A.B. Smith put his second shot on the par 4 second hole within inches of the cup and made the putt to register a 3. Smith and his playing partners called that one-under score a birdie. Smith also claimed to have coined the term "eagle" for any score of two under par. A double eagle (also known as an albatross) is apropos, since scoring one is as rare a feat as sighting the bird made famous in Samuel T. Coleridge's epic poem "The Rime of the Ancient Mariner."

Long before "birdie" entered the golf lexicon, "bogey" was linked with the game's first scoring system. It was not until 1891 that the idea of standardizing the number of shots each golf hole should take was initiated. This notion was proposed by Hugh Rotherham, who suggested the term "ground score" for what is now called par. This became the norm in matches. During one particular competition in this era, someone exclaimed about one of the participants, "This player of yours is a regular Bogey man!"

Eventually, by the middle of the twentieth century, the word was adopted to mean any score one over par. Speaking of par, as a golf term, the word comes from the stock exchange usage where a stock could be above or below its normal or "par" figure.

And what about the origins of "fore," that four-letter word you hope never to hear yelled by anyone near you during your round? This one is believed to have Scottish origins. While the exact etymology is not known for sure, the *Oxford English Dictionary* records the first use in relation to golf in 1878. Defining it as a warning cry to golfers, the dictionary states that it was a truncation of the word "before." Still, there are several other theories on the word's origin in the game. The most plausible is that it comes from the use of forecaddies (those who walked ahead of players and stood where golf balls landed to help players spot their balls — and not lose as many). Players would yell to warn these spotters of an approaching errant shot and eventually this warning was shortened from forecaddie to fore!

PASSPORT PLEASE!

Anything to declare? Just the yips,* a slice, and a golf bag filled with well-worn Titleist Pro V1 balls. What about your handicap — be honest! Such queries are not the usual ones you would expect to get asked before arriving at your local golf course, unless you are at one of the five courses that cross international borders. Imagine the possibility that an errant shot off the tee not only lands out-of-bounds, but out of the country — or even in another time zone!

At the semi-private Aroostock Valley Country Club in Fort Fairfield, Maine, the Maple Leaf and the Stars and Stripes fly side by side on the club's pole and both appear

---

* The "yips" is a word golfers hate to hear. It refers to a neurological condition that causes the brain to distort the message being sent to the muscles; it is suffered by some golfers as involuntary wrist spasms right before they strike the ball.

on its crest. An old rusty sign near the pro shop proclaims: "Avoid Penalty — Report to Customs — Vehicles Entering the United States Must Be Reported." The nine-hole course was founded in 1929 in the remote borderland straddling the Maine and New Brunswick border by a group of thirsty New Englanders. It was the Prohibition era and liquor was banned throughout America, but not in Canada. By building their clubhouse across the border, these gentlemen made sure they could enjoy a libation with more kick after their round.

By 1960, the course had added an additional nine holes. Pull your opening shot too far to the left, and a drive that started in Canada might end up in America. In 2020, during the global pandemic, when the borders between Canada and the United States closed to prevent the spread of Covid-19, Canadians could not play, since entry to the club is located on the American side.

The Gateway Cities Golf Club, which spans Saskatchewan and North Dakota, also shares a border between Canada and the United States. The clubhouse for this nine-hole course is located on the American side, while most of the holes are located in Canada. For a long time, the international boundary was loosely marked on a gravel road. During the pandemic, the U.S. Customs and Border Protection Agency had to temporarily close this makeshift crossing and install video cameras to track anyone trying to enter America for a game of golf.

North American courses are not the only ones that share an international border. There are a trio in Europe that also share this feature. Llanymynech Golf Club shares a border between England and Wales: fifteen holes are in the Welsh-speaking country and three are in England. Adding to the distinctiveness of this border course, on the fourth hole, you tee off in Wales and putt out in England.

International Golf Maastricht shares a border between Holland and Belgium. The routing of this course is even more unusual than many other courses that straddle the borders of countries, since the holes are not evenly divided; the first seven holes are in Holland while the next five (holes eight through twelve) are located in Belgium. Golfers then finish their round back in the Netherlands.

The Tornio Golf Club (also known as Meri-Lapin Golfklubi) shares a border between Finland and Sweden. Eleven holes are in Sweden and seven holes are in Finland. What makes the Tornio GC even more interesting is that it not only crosses a border, but also a time zone. That happens on the sixth hole, a par 3, when once your ball is airborne, it travels through a time zone before arriving on the green.

THE LONGEST WALK

Slow play normally drives me — and most golfers — nuts. And it lessens the enjoyment and the serenity the game offers. But if I ever have a chance to go Down Under and play Nullarbor Links, my attitude toward pace of play, at least while there, would change.

Forget the North American average of four hours and thirty minutes for a round. To play eighteen holes at Nullarbor, four days minimum is required. Located along the southern coast of Australia, this "walk" is 1,385 kilometres long and crosses two Australian states — meandering through plains and past historical landmarks where golfers not only have fun but also learn about the rich cultural history and the earliest settlers of the Australian Outback.

Two buddies, over a bottle of red wine one night, conjured up this dream as a way to bring more tourism to this rural region. The concept: construct one hole in each town (or near a roadhouse) along the desolate Eyre Highway that links Western and South Australia via the Nullarbor Plain. Officially opened in 2009, the course begins — and ends — in the gold mining town of Kalgoorlie and is officially the world's longest golf course. The average distance between holes is sixty-six kilometres; two of its holes are nearly two hundred kilometres apart.

On the "fairways," it is suggested golfers tee up their shots, since the area between tee and green consists of the Outback's natural terrain and is pretty rugged. One hole is situated on a working sheep station. Windmills dot another. In between trying to make par, take an overnight rest at the Balladonia Hotel Motel. The lodging includes a museum that, along with sharing knowledge about the Aboriginal heritage of the area and local flora and fauna, tells the story of how NASA's Skylab space station landed on the site back in 1979 when it re-entered the earth's atmosphere.

Nullarbor was created so that visitors could take in these cultural experiences. So sightsee and linger for as little — or as long — as you like after playing each hole. Enjoy Pacific oysters. Surf at the world-famous Cactus Beach. Or explore caves where you might encounter a dingo or a wedge-tailed eagle gnawing on its dinner. Other wildlife you might spot during your round includes wombats, emus, kangaroos, and three different species of poisonous snakes.

Don't forget to drink lots of water and take breaks as temperatures can reach 50°C. Make sure your scorecard is stamped after each hole to receive a certificate that proclaims you completed the world's longest golf course. Since opening, the course has hosted an annual tournament called Chasing the Sun; the ten-day event attracts enthusiastic golfers from around the world.

HAIR TO FEATHERS AND SO MUCH BETTER

Though most Scots refute the claim, it is said that a precursor to golf was played with a wooden ball. And while no examples of wooden balls have ever been found in Scotland, there definitely existed many other early variants of this essential piece of equipment, from a hand-sewn sack filled with hair to one filled with feathers. The history of the golf ball, a mass-produced item that supports a $1-billion-industry today, is fascinating.

Following the wooden ball, which did not travel far and broke when struck too hard, arrived the hairy ball. A bit dirty sounding, perhaps. For the first century of golf in Scotland, these hairy golf balls, made of hand-sewn leather filled with cattle hair or straw, were the most common. Most of these were imported from the Netherlands. Agriculture was booming in Holland in the fourteenth century, and its exports to Britain rose significantly. Those exports included thousands of sacks of wool and tens of thousands of hides. These balls were cheap to manufacture and remained popular even after the invention of the feathery — the next step in the golf ball's evolution.

The feathery was harder and more durable than the hairy because although the leather contracted as it dried, the feathers expanded. The construction of a feathery was similar to the hairy, but instead of being filled with cow hair, they were stuffed with goose or chicken feathers. The feathery had several drawbacks: a) if it got wet, the feathery fell apart; b) it was hard to make the balls round; and c) they were expensive, since their manufacture required a lot of labour — it took several hours to manufacture just one ball, so the earliest craftsmen could only produce a few balls each day. This is the primary reason golf remained a game enjoyed mostly by the well-to-do for the first couple of centuries after its invention.

A Scottish-American man of the cloth invented the next iteration of the golf ball in 1848, and it became the one that opened up the game to the middle classes. Rev. Dr. Robert Adams Paterson made a ball stuffed with gutta percha packing material — a milky latex substance that came from the sap of a tree found throughout Malaysia. The gutta percha, or "guttie" as it was called, was more durable than the feathery, it was water-resistant and, since there was an abundance of this substance readily available in this former British colony, it was cheaper to make.

Similar was the Haskell, invented at the turn of the twentieth century by New England bicycle manufacturer Coburn Haskell. He filled the core of the ball with solid rubber. By accident, golfers discovered the more nicks they had in their ball, the smoother and more consistent its flight. This discovery eventually led to the creation of dimples in the ball. Today, the average ball has 336 little indentations that improve airflow — leading to more control and a better, more consistent trajectory.

The golf ball manufacturing business is big business. It's estimated 1.2 billion of these orbs are manufactured annually, and the average golfer goes through a hundred balls each year. Dedicated teams of engineers work in labs studying ways to enhance ball flight and performance, especially the distance a ball can travel. This quest for distance in golf ball technology (and also clubs) has made many long holes that once were considered a challenge much easier for professional golfers, who average drives close to three hundred yards. The golf ball R&D team at segment leader Titleist includes more than seventy chemists, physicists, mathematicians, engineers, and other specialists.

Some believe that things have gone too far, as the distances professionals can now hit a ball are absurd. Golf's governing bodies certainly believe this to be the case. In late 2023, they announced a plan to manage this problem. To reduce the distances that balls will fly — especially when hit with a driver — the ruling bodies have decreed that certain changes need to be made. The plan involves new standards for golf balls and changes in testing parameters (increase in clubhead speed, lower spin and launch). All balls must conform to these new standards by January 1, 2030. For the average player, the reduction in distance resulting from these changes is expected to be minimal (about five yards). So, go ahead and grip it and rip it as if nothing has changed.

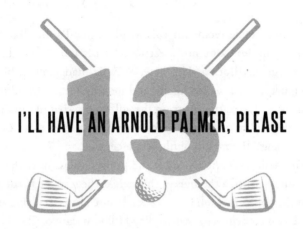

I'LL HAVE AN ARNOLD PALMER, PLEASE

There are different levels of fame. Take Arnold Palmer. Known in golfing circles as the King (sixty-two professional wins might have something to do with him being given this regal nickname), Palmer started chasing the white ball as a three-year-old rug rat at Latrobe Country Club in Pennsylvania, where his father was the club's professional. The first professional golfer to win $1 million in career earnings, Palmer used some of these winnings to buy Latrobe.

Palmer was well loved — his devout fans at PGA Tour tournaments were known as Arnie's Army — long before he created a drink we now call an Arnold Palmer. But that homemade concoction, which has become a thirst quencher for golfers and non-golfers alike, certainly adds to his legacy.

The simple recipe for this drink struck Palmer like a lightning bolt one hot afternoon at his home in Palm Springs, California. His wife, Winnie, had made a big pitcher of iced tea for lunch, and looking for a refreshing drink after sweating away on the golf course that morning, he decided to add some lemonade to the pitcher as an experiment. The mix, roughly 75 percent tea and 25 percent lemonade, was, he decided, the perfect thirst quencher. Palmer packed a thermos of this drink whenever he headed to the golf course, and he also made sure it was available at the two golf clubs he owned: Bay Hill in Orlando, Florida, and Latrobe.

One day, when he ordered this homemade drink at a restaurant in Palm Springs, a woman at a nearby table overheard his request and said to the waitress, "I'll have what he's having. I want an Arnold Palmer." After that, the drink started to catch on via word of mouth.

Palmer did not consider marketing this blended refresher until the early 1990s. The first attempts failed when it was time to go to market. Finally, in 2001, Orlando businessman Chris Byrd, who lived near Bay Hill, presented a winning marketing proposal to Palmer. Byrd created a management company called Innovative Flavors. Eventually, Byrd and Palmer struck a licensing and manufacturing deal with Arizona Beverages to sell a 650-mL can of the drink Palmer originally created in his kitchen solely for his enjoyment.

Following its launch, Arizona saw multiple years of 100 percent growth. Today, there are eight flavours in the Arnold Palmer line of beverages, and Arizona iced tea produces more than four hundred million cans annually.

The last word about his namesake drink goes to the man himself. In *A Life Well Played: My Stories*, the King writes, "I'm often asked what I think when people order an Arnold Palmer in front of me. Frankly, I'm a little embarrassed, but I'm happy they're ordering it. I like to think that maybe I've created something that is fun. And it has been fun for me. I have one or two every day. And when I order it, I just say, 'I'll have a Palmer.'"

THE TEXAS TRAILBLAZER

A trailblazer, like few athletes seen before or since. Meet Babe Zaharias: an inspiration to women of her generation — and today — for her athletic accomplishments in a male-dominated sport.

Babe was named the Associated Press Athlete of the Year six times, and their writers later voted her "the greatest female athlete of the twentieth century."

Born Mildred Ella Didrikson in the coastal city of Port Arthur, Texas, she excelled at every sport she tried, including baseball, basketball, track and field, hockey, tennis, swimming and diving, billiards, and even bowling. As a teenager, Didrikson already had big dreams, declaring, "I want to be the greatest athlete who ever lived."

Wonder why this golf pioneer shares a nickname with the greatest baseball player that ever lived — the Sultan of Swat, George Herman "Babe" Ruth? She was labelled Babe by her mom one afternoon when she smashed five home runs in a Little League baseball game.

Before she ever wowed spectators in golf exhibitions and tournaments across North America, a twenty-one-year-old Babe qualified in not just one but five track and field events for the 1932 Olympics. However, rules allowed women to compete in only three events. At the Los Angeles Games, Babe won gold in two of the three events she entered (javelin and 80-metre hurdles, where she set a world record of 11.7 seconds) and added silver in the high jump. Two years later, she pitched four innings with three major league baseball teams during spring training and set another record that still stands: the farthest baseball throw by a woman — 296 feet.

Babe's Olympic performance so impressed sportswriter Grantland Rice that he raved about what he had witnessed: "She is beyond belief until you see her perform. Then you finally understand that you are looking at the most flawless section of muscle harmony, of complete mental and physical coordination the world of sport has ever known." After the Olympics, Babe was one of the most famous people in the United States.

The following year, golf became Babe's sport of choice — and the one she is most remembered for. Thanks to Rice, she received an invitation to play a round with three other sportswriters at Brentwood Country Club. She shot 91, regularly smashed the ball 250 yards off the tee, and immediately fell in love with the game.

In 1938 Babe was the first woman to compete in a PGA Tour event against men when she qualified for the Los Angeles Open. She did not make the cut that time, but seven years later, she did — an achievement that has not been repeated since. Covering the PGA Tour tournament Babe played, Braven Dyer of the *Los Angeles Times* wrote about the significance of her opening-round 76: "This may not sound so amazing, but she beat eighty-four males who were out there hacking away."

Asked once by a reporter how she consistently drove the ball some 250 yards though she was only five-foot-seven and didn't weigh more than 145 pounds, she replied, "You've got to loosen your girdle and let 'er fly!"

In 1948 Babe became the first woman to qualify for the U.S. Open but was denied entry in the event because the organizers (the United States Golf Association) declared the major tournament was "only open to men." The following year, she helped co-found the Ladies Professional Golf Association (LPGA).

Gender discrimination — especially in sports — was widespread during Babe's life. Not all reporters were as impressed with Babe's charm and athletic prowess as Rice.

For example, Joe Williams opined in a *New York World-Telegram* piece that "it would be much better if she and her ilk stayed at home, got themselves prettied up and waited for the phone to ring." Another reporter posed a question in print, tongue firmly planted in his cheek, "What bathroom should she use, 'Mr.' 'Miss' or 'It'?"

Once Babe started to golf, it did not take long for her to dominate; she hit as many as 1,500 balls a day and the practice paid off. Over the course of an illustrious eighteen-year career, she won eighty-two tournaments, including fourteen amateur events in a row during one stretch; Babe was also the first American to win the British Ladies Amateur. The greatest year of her professional career came in 1950. She led the money list, winning ten tournaments faster than any other golfer in LPGA history, which included the three considered the Grand Slam of women's golf: the U.S. Open, the Titleholders Championship, and the Women's Western Open.

Babe's life was cut short when she passed away at forty-five years old following a courageous battle with colon cancer. Today, in Beaumont, Texas, a museum honors Babe's legacy, which forever changed the landscape of women's sports.

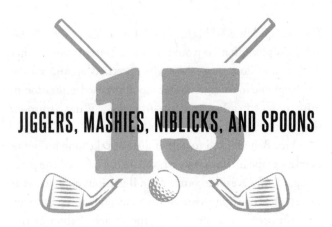

JIGGERS, MASHIES, NIBLICKS, AND SPOONS

Before golf clubs had numbers to indicate their loft, the game's earliest equipment, now called antiques or hickory clubs, had some pretty unusual names, which reflected their purpose and use. From hickory to persimmon wood to forged steel-shafted and graphite clubs, what a long, strange trip the evolution of golf clubs has been.

First up in this lexicon lesson: the antique clubs with wood heads. The "long club" or "play club" is equivalent to today's driver, so named as it was used to "play away" from the tee. Next up is the "brassie." This club, most similar to a modern-day 2- or 3-wood, got its name because a brass plate was welded onto its sole. Then there's the "cleek" (like a modern 4-wood), the "spoon" (like a modern 5-wood), and finally the "baffie" (or "baffling spoon"), like today's 7-wood or hybrid club.

Some of these pre-modern clubs had wood shafts but iron heads. The cleek was a driving iron that one could also use to putt as it looked like a blade with no loft. There was also a group of clubs known as "mashies": the "mid-mashie" (3-iron); the "mashie iron" (4-iron); the "mashie" (5-iron equivalent); "spade mashie" (6-iron); "mashie niblick" (7-iron); "pitching niblick" (like an 8-iron); and the "niblick" (like a 9-iron). After mashie and niblick, one of the funniest names given to early golf clubs is probably "jigger" — used for chip shots.

Today, societies exist in North America devoted to preserving these hickory-shafted sticks. These associations, like the Golf Heritage Society in the United States (founded in 1970) and the Golf Historical Society of Canada (founded in 1988), hold several tournaments each year. In those, it's all about the wood and trying to recapture that feeling of what it was like to play a couple of hundred years ago when the Scots invented the game. Players fill their bags with mashies, niblicks, and jiggers and even dress the part — eschewing modern styles for a newsboy cap, knickerbockers, and ties that were the popular fashion on the links of yesteryear.

THE ONE-LINER KING

Sporting a Panama hat and wearing loud outfits, long before such styles became popular in golf, Juan "Chi Chi" Rodriguez was one of the most colourful characters in professional golf. The charismatic gentleman was also known for his zingers, one-liners like the one describing his childhood home: "It was so small that there wasn't enough room for him to change his mind."

Rodriguez was raised in a family of six kids in Rio Piedras, a poor neighbourhood on the outskirts of San Juan, Puerto Rico. He learned his work ethic from his dad, a labourer and cattle handler who worked fourteen-hour days, six or seven days a week in hot and dusty sugar cane fields. At eight years old, Juan was hired as a forecaddie at the local golf course, where he caddied for eleven years before entering the army. His nickname was bestowed on him when he was twelve years old, and it stuck. The young Rodriguez ran around the ballpark one day telling everyone he was his idol, Chi Chi Flores, the Puerto Rican baseball star.

A self-taught golfer, he had an unorthodox swing, the legacy of a boyhood spent practising by hitting a tin can with a branch from a guava tree. Despite standing only five feet and seven inches and weighing in at 135 pounds soaking wet, Chi Chi was one of the longest hitters of his era. From 1963 to 1979, the Puerto Rican won eight times on the PGA Tour. Before retiring from professional golf, he added another twenty-two titles during seven years playing on the Seniors circuit. Rodriguez is the only Puerto Rican to be inducted into the World Golf Hall of Fame.

Above all, the high-school dropout was a showman. Rodriguez played to win but he also wanted to entertain the fans. This flamboyant play was most in view when Rodriguez drained a long putt and did a toreador routine. Upon hearing his ball drop into the cup, the Puerto Rican wielded his putter like a sword, and after completing an imaginary coup de grâce, he sheathed his "weapon" into an imaginary scabbard.

Where did the sword dance come from? Originally, Chi Chi's shtick was placing his Panama hat over the hole after sinking a birdie or eagle putt, supposedly so the ball wouldn't pop out. While the fans lapped up this routine, Rodriguez's fellow pros were not so amused, complaining this gimmick was damaging the hole. So, figuring a fine putting performance mimics that of a matador in a bull-ring, he came up with the idea of the sword dance — the hole was a bull, so once the ball dropped, he had slain his adversary and proceeded to wave his weapon (his putter) to flaunt his prowess.

Despite not being golf fans, the new wave band Devo were fascinated by Chi Chi's prowess, fashion statements, and his shtick on the course. The story goes that while a pair of the band members were shopping through a Kmart one afternoon, the photo on the label of a package of practice balls caught their attention. The photo showing Rodriguez with a giant golf ball behind him that "loomed up like a manic moon" made such an impression that Devo later used a copy of this image on the sleeve of its first U.K. single, "Be Stiff." The band then signed to Warner Brothers Records in the United States; not having time to wait for Rodriguez's permission to use his likeness, the record label's marketing department made alterations to the image's mouth, nose, facial shape, and eyes so it did not look exactly like the Puerto Rican golfer.

The "ebullient showman" and "the golf world's swash-buckling champion" died on August 8, 2024, at the age of eighty-eight.

RULES, RULES, RULES

Hit a ball off a tee and put it in a hole hundreds of yards away in as few shots as you can. For a game with such a simple-sounding goal, why so many rules? It was not always the case.

The Scots invented this grand old game, and in 1744, a group known as the Gentlemen Golfers of Leith drafted its first set of rules. Known as the "Articles and Laws in the Playing at Golf," these thirteen guidelines were established for the Silver Club tournament played at Leith Links in Edinburgh, Scotland. These articles were preserved in the club's minute book and more widely adopted when, a decade later, they were used for a similar tournament at St. Andrews. Today, the original list of golf rules is housed in the National Library of Scotland.

Those thirteen guidelines, which fit on one large page, mostly remain in place. Over the years, there has been some wordsmithing — and a few amendments have been made to these original rules. But as the game evolved, the number of rules has increased significantly — peaking at thirty-four before golf's governing bodies streamlined them to twenty-four. However, each rule has many subsets. As a result, the printed version of today's official *Rules of Golf* runs to more than 240 pages. Quite a hefty book.

There are now so many rules, subsets, and sub-subsets that even professional players do not always know — let alone understand — them all. That's why every PGA Tour tournament has up to ten rules officials on site to help with any disputed or confusing on-course rulings.

•

Unfortunately, a rule almost caused Sergio Garcia to lose his only major title. It happened during the final round of the 2017 Masters tournament. The trouble started on Augusta National's thirteenth hole. Tied with Justin Rose for the lead, Garcia hit a tee shot that went out of bounds, requiring him to declare an unplayable lie, drop a new ball, and take a one-shot penalty. That's when the controversy occurred. Garcia dropped his ball in some pine needles and before hitting his shot moved some of the loose needles away from his ball. Some TV viewers (today's unofficial arbitrators of the rules) called CBS Sports claiming Garcia's ball had moved when he moved the needles. According to Rule 18-2, if a player causes his ball to move, he incurs a one-stroke penalty and must return the ball to its original position.

The golf gods must have been smiling on the Spaniard that day. The Augusta National Golf Club rules committee reviewed the video and determined Garcia's ball had not moved, so no additional penalty was assessed. Garcia and Justin Rose ended up in a playoff to decide the winner. Imagine if that ruling had gone the other way? Maybe Garcia would still be pining for a Green Jacket rather than having one hanging in his closet.

•

Here are some of modern golf's more unusual rules.

Do you love teeing it up early in the morning like me? Are you a dew sweeper — always looking to secure the first tee time of the day right behind the maintenance crew? Go ahead and enjoy these crack of dawn games, but make sure you don't mess with that moisture on your Pro V1. According to Rule 13-2, you cannot wipe dew off your ball. If you do, it's a two-stroke penalty.

Rule 23-6 says that you cannot move a live snake if you encounter one on the course. I'm terrified of snakes, and

I've actually encountered them several times in my playing career. (I came across one once when I was playing the Old White course at the Greenbrier in West Virginia. Luckily, I had a caddie with me, so I let him encourage the massive black rat snake slithering in the grass to move along.) Why is this a rule? Apparently, snakes, like any reptiles (including alligators) you find on the course, are considered an "outside agency." Oh, and a humorous addition to this rule: if the snake is dead, it becomes "a loose impediment" and you can move it without penalty.

Another strange rule outlines what to do if your ball lands on an orange or any piece of fruit. Say what? Well, it must have happened to someone at some time, or Rule 23-10, which states that you must play the ball and/or fruit as it lies or declare an unplayable and take a one-stroke penalty, would not have been written. How about if your ball ends up under a parked car? Rule 24-1/24-2b covers this rare occurrence. If you find yourself in this situation, you can either have the car moved or get a free drop.

You might think that if you smacked your playing partner with your ball it would be a penalty. But no! Golf etiquette does, however, dictate that you should yell "fore" to warn anyone in the landing zone of an errant shot before it strikes them.

Finally, here is a rule if you golf at a desert course where cacti border the rough. If you land next to one of these plants and your swing is impeded, can you move your ball? No, but the kind folks who wrote up the subset to Rule 1-2/10 offer a solution to deal with this prickly situation: you can wrap your arm or leg in a towel to protect it from the cactus spines. What if your ball gets embedded in a cactus? It happens more than you might think. I saw many saguaro cacti scarred by what looked like bullet holes when I played in Arizona. The rules say you have to claim a lost ball, drop another one at the nearest point of relief, and take a one-stroke penalty.

What would those early Scots — and the Gentlemen Golfers of Leith — think if they knew how complicated the guidelines to the game they invented had become?

HOGAN THE HERO

After almost dying in a horrific crash when his car collided with a bus, Ben Hogan not only returned to play professional golf again but also won another eleven tournaments, including five majors.

In the wee hours on Groundhog Day (February 2, 1949), Hogan and his wife, Valerie, were driving home to Fort Worth, Texas, from Phoenix, Arizona, where he had lost in a tournament to Jimmy Demaret.

Crossing a small one-way bridge, Hogan, thirty-six years old, had no time to avoid the Greyhound bus that barrelled toward him. He dove across his wife's body as the impact occurred to try to protect her. As a result of his courageous act, Valerie was left with only minor injuries. The reigning champion of both the U.S. Open and PGA

Championship was not so fortunate, suffering a broken left ankle, contusions to his left leg, a broken collarbone, a cracked rib, a double fracture of the pelvis, a head abrasion, and internal injuries. It took more than ninety minutes for an ambulance to arrive. Doctors feared the worst — initially not even sure he would survive, they believed that if he did, chances were good he might never walk again.

Hogan spent fifty-nine days in an El Paso hospital, and during this time, blood clots on his left leg broke off and entered his lung. Again, the prognosis was dire. But a specialist from Tulane arrived in time to perform a two-hour operation that saved his life.

Miraculously, Hogan arrived home on April 1 and by the following month he was already back on a golf course. First, just as a spectator. He admitted to reporters that he was unsure whether of all the injuries, his broken collarbone would permit him to swing a golf club again.

On December 10, Hogan played his first eighteen holes, a round at Colonial Country Club, a little over eleven months since that near-fatal car accident. By January 1950, he was back competing on the PGA Tour, where he played well enough to force a playoff with Sam Snead, which he lost. Just a few months later — and a mere sixteen months from those life-threatening injuries — Hogan hoisted another major trophy, when he beat Lloyd Mangrum and

George Fazio in an eighteen-hole playoff to win the U.S. Open at Merion Golf Club in Ardmore, Pennsylvania.

The Texan, who the press now dubbed the "mechanical man," added five more major titles (two Masters, two more U.S. Opens, and the 1953 British Open Championship at Carnoustie Golf Links in Angus, Scotland). Still, one wonders how many more tournaments Ben might have won without the chronic leg problems that resulted from this accident. Despite the fact that Hogan remained one of the game's top players, only eleven of his sixty-four titles came after 1949.

The Golf Writers Association of America pays tribute to the Texan's bravery with the Ben Hogan Award, which is given annually to a golfer who has stayed active in golf despite a physical handicap or serious illness. Hogan's story is truly inspiring — one of the greatest comebacks in sports history.

FAIRWAY FASHION

When the Scots dressed for a game on the links, fashion was not considered. The courses where the earliest Scottish games were played were windy and cold. These early golfers dressed solely with comfort and warmth in mind; hence, wool and tweed were the favoured fabrics. Modern fashion on the fairways is all about style.

A quick history lesson on the evolution of golf fashion. It was in the Roaring Twenties, a decade of decadence in America, that golf fashion for men became more stylish and elegant. The most common attire was a single-breasted grey suit. Knitted short or lightweight slacks were also worn. The knickerbockers worn by those early Scots evolved to become even shorter, baggier pants (known as plus fours). These were worn with wool socks. A tweed cap and necktie completed the outfit.

In the 1930s and 1940s, as golf exploded in popularity in the United States, the strict fashion rules adopted by the wealthy players were loosened. The new middle-class players preferred more casual, lightweight clothing. It comes as no surprise that in the 1950s, the same decade that colour TV was introduced, the palette displayed by the rest of the world became more vibrant. This is when golf fashion started its slow march away from the neutral whites and greys and tans that had dominated the early years of the game, adopting coloured fabrics for both shirts and trousers.

The 1970s, especially the early part of the decade, were a groovy time for fashion, and the wild styles of the hippies' attire found their way onto the links. New colours like purple, magenta, and green became popular choices.

Today, golf fashion is big business. Even if you yourself are not particularly choosy about what you wear, you are sure to see many fashionistas during your round. Many golfers seem as concerned with their appearance on the course as they are about their final score. Today, there is a fashion style to match any personality. For those that like to stand out and make a statement, there are brands like Loudmouth that feature, as the name suggests, big, bold coloured pants, shorts, and shirts.

Fashion on the fairways in the twenty-first century also focuses on performance-enhancing apparel. Clothes are designed with modern technology that allows them to breathe (circulating air more freely throughout the garment). New fabrics that are not just comfortable, allowing for maximum mobility, but also lightweight and "moisture-wicking" — they help to hold sweat away from the skin — have been developed.

Adidas and Nike are the leading apparel brands, but there are now hundreds of options from which to choose: the makers of luxury brands and designer apparel all see the revenue potential in this market segment. Research forecasts that the global golf apparel market will surpass $4 billion in 2027.

WHAT IN THE WORD?

Scots discovered many things in a variety of indus-tries from science and technology to agriculture and the arts. The pedal bicycle, the telephone, the television, and penicillin are just a few of the gifts that Scottish-born inventors have bestowed on the world.

While Scots invented the grand old game of golf, the word "golf" originated in the Netherlands, where the first golf balls were manufactured. Some scholars believe the Dutch played a game of "kolf," a distant cousin to golf, with a stick and a ball on the frozen canals. And no, the tale told by some that golf is an acronym for "gentlemen only, ladies forbidden" is definitely not true. The fact that Mary, Queen of Scots was a keen golfer alone dispels this misogynistic myth.

The etymology of the English noun "golf" derived linguistically from the Dutch word for club: *kolf* or *kolve*. As the Scots became passionate about the new game, their dialect made this Dutch word morph into *goff* or *gouff* ... both meaning a stick. It's interesting to note that before the first dictionaries were printed and published, words did not have standardized spelling, so people wrote phonetically. Hence the differences in early examples of this word in print. The word appeared as early as the fifteenth century in Scottish writings; the first documented mention of the word "golf" is in Edinburgh on March 6, 1457, when King James II banned "ye golf," in an attempt to encourage archery practice, which citizens were neglecting in favour of this new pastime.

THE RENAISSANCE GRAND SLAM MAN

Robert Tyre Jones Jr. was an entrepreneur, a schol-
ar, and one of the greatest amateur golfers to ever play the
game. Better known as Bobby Jones, this gentleman from
Georgia remains the only player to ever win golf's Grand
Slam in the same season. When Jones dominated the sport
from the mid 1920s to the mid 1930s, this Slam consisted
of the British Amateur, the British Open, the U.S. Amateur,
and the U.S. Open.* In 1930 Jones won all four of those
championships. As an amateur, he did not win any official
prize money in the two professional events, but he did pocket
$60,000 from a British bookie after completing the feat, since
Jones bet on himself, at 50 to 1 odds, to win the Grand Slam.

---

* The modern Grand Slam, which no one has won, includes four major golf
championships: the Masters, the U.S. Open, the British Open, and the PGA
Championship.

Beyond the Grand Slam, Jones achieved a great many other successes. He played in thirty-one golf championships and placed first or second in more than 50 percent of them. And he did all of that before "retiring" from competitive golf before he was thirty, after dominating the amateur ranks and even regularly beating some of the top professionals of his era, like Walter Hagen and Gene Sarazen. On the decision to put his competitive golf days behind him, Jones said, "[Championship golf] is something like a cage. First, you are expected to get into it, and then you are expected to stay there. But of course, nobody can stay there."

Jones's putter is also one of the most famous pieces of equipment in modern golf history. Jim Maiden, a Scotsman who emigrated to the United States and became the head golf professional at Nassau Country Club on Long Island, owned this putter and let Jones borrow it for the first time at the 1920 U.S. Amateur. The story is that Jones sank eight consecutive putts the first time he tried Calamity Jane*; he left the course with it and went on to use this short, light hickory-shafted putter to win thirteen major championships in just seven years. Today, the original Calamity Jane is on display in the clubhouse of Augusta National. Only two other players in the history of

---

* Maiden gave the putter its moniker — Calamity Jane — after the American frontierswoman and sharpshooter Martha "Calamity Jane" Canary, figuring anyone wielding this flatstick would putt with the same accuracy as the notorious Wild West character.

the game have won more majors: Jack Nicklaus (eighteen) and Tiger Woods (fifteen).

His Augusta National course score of sixty-four in 1936, the second year of the tournament, remained a record for fifty years. Jones co-founded Augusta National Golf Club and the idea for the Masters Tournament with his friend, New York City stockbroker and investor Clifford Roberts.

A true Renaissance man, Jones studied English literature at Harvard and then obtained a law degree at Emory University — he joined his father's law firm after being called to the bar and practised civil and contract law until his death in 1971. If that was not enough, Jones was also an entrepreneur. In 1932 he designed a set of woods and the first ever matched set of irons for A.G. Spalding. Later, he started and owned Coca-Cola bottling companies in New England, Michigan, Scotland, Uruguay, Argentina, and Chile.

Although he never took any formal lessons himself, Jones became a teacher, making a series of instructional short films for golfers, focusing on various parts of the game. Finally, the golfer received not just one but two ticker-tape parades in his honour in New York City.

GET A GRIP

One of the first things one is taught in a golf lesson is how to grip the club. The reason why was explained perfectly by legendary Texas golf instructor Harvey Penick when he replied to a question by writer Bud Shrake, who worked with him to pen his bestselling book.

"Why is the grip so important?" Shrake asked.

"Well, it controls everything," Penick replied. "When a pupil compensates for a bad grip, he gets bad aim. If you make a mistake going back, to offset a bad grip, you've got to make a mistake going down, to offset that one."

According to the official *Rules of Golf*, there is no right way to hold a club. But there are three ways to hold the club that have become commonly used. The Vardon or overlap grip (the most common grip, used by 90 percent of PGA

Tour players and the majority of amateurs) is named after British golf professional Harry Vardon. In this grip, your hands are connected through the right pinky finger, which lies on top of the depression between the left hand's index and middle fingers. The interlock grip is the second most popular grip and is used by both Jack Nicklaus and Tiger Woods. Here, both hands once again connect via the right hand's pinky finger and the left hand's index finger, but those fingers cross rather than sit one on top of the other. The other commonly used grip is the ten-finger, neutral — or baseball — grip, which is exactly what it sounds like: you grip the club with all ten fingers touching the club, in the same fashion as one grips a baseball bat.

•

The word "grip" can act as a verb, but it can also be used as a noun — the wrap around the shaft of a golf club is called a grip. The earliest wooden clubs did not have any grips. Scottish golf pioneers wore a pair of gloves to protect their hands from the hickory-shafted clubs. These also allowed them to improve their grip, ensuring that the sticks did not fly out of their hands when they swung them. At some point, early Scottish sheep farmers who enjoyed a game of golf started wrapping leather around their wooden clubs to give them a better feel.

Elver Lamkin worked by day with Chicago Rawhide, a company that tanned and treated leather for industrial uses and later the automotive industry. In 1925 Lamkin, taking a lesson from the Scots, started to craft premium leather grips for golf clubs in the garage of his suburban Chicago home. The story goes that Wilson Sporting Goods set up a meeting one day with Chicago Rawhide and asked if they could help develop a leather wrap on a golf club. The company wasn't interested, but Lamkin, an avid golfer, who was in that meeting, raised his hand and told Wilson he would give it a go. He succeeded and Wilson Sporting Goods became the first company to manufacture golf grips in the United States.

In 1953 Westgate Rubber Company of Akron, Ohio, started to manufacture a slip-on rubber grip, marketed under the name Golf Pride. Simple technology to modern eyes, but it was a revolutionary invention for club-making and the sport at that time. This slip-on grip became the new standard. In 1958 Tommy Bolt, signed by Golf Pride to endorse its new product, won the U.S. Open — the first win in a major by a player using the new slip-on grip.

With the introduction of slip-on rubber grips, leather grips took a back seat. Lamkin felt the rubber grip was just a fad and refused to transition his business away from leather. He was finally convinced to change his mind by his son Robert, however, and Lamkin started to manufacture both leather and rubber grips. Lamkin, a family business run by the fourth generation of Lamkins, is still around, making grips that are among the most popular today. However Golf Pride is the number one grip provider to the golf industry.

More than 80 percent of PGA Tour players use Golf Pride's Tour Velvet grips, which include Plus4 technology. The grip's soft material provides the feel of four extra layers of tape on the lower half of the grip; with it, players can lighten their grip pressure and the tension in their hands and arms, which leads to a freer swing and often bigger distance gains.

BAH, HUMBUG! I'M BUNKERED

Modern golfers often prefer having their ball land in a bunker rather than in the rough. Thanks to improvements in design and technology, modern wedges have the right weight and bounce to cut through the sand in these traps, making this once difficult shot pretty routine. Perhaps that's not always the case for the average golfer, but things are definitely better these days. But why did these dreaded hazards develop anyway?

In Scotland, bunkers, or sand traps as they are now usually called, were non-existent when the game was invented. When these appeared on the earliest links courses,*

---

* Links courses, the original type of course, are found mainly in Wales, Scotland, England, and Ireland. They are typically located in sandy soil along a seacoast. Such courses feature naturally formed contours and undulations such as rolling dunes. Deep, rugged rough and pot bunkers are also common features.

it was more by accident than by design — the sheep who grazed on the grounds would huddle up and burrow into the ground to protect themselves from the wind and rain off the fierce North Sea storms that often buffeted the area. The groundcover in the areas where they huddled would be destroyed, and the sand and stone underneath would be exposed. As golf course design developed, the earliest architects decided to keep these hazards and built sand bunkers into their designs to punish poor shots. As Willie Park Jr., the famed Scottish golf professional and designer, once wrote: "If a bunker is visible to the player, and there is sufficient room to avoid it, it is the player's responsibility to steer clear of it."

The use of bunkering as both an aesthetic element — a way to shape holes — and also as a feature that adds an extra layer of difficulty to a course became common in the modern era of golf design and construction. The term "sand trap" originated in 1922, an expression shouted frequently by frustrated golfers whose balls ended up in a bunker, who cursed their creation.

24 GOLF AU NATUREL

Not for prudes, only for nudes! La Jenny naturist course, near Bordeaux, France, is a six-hole course inside what is described as a "family park." What makes this course different — and the number one reason you won't find my family vacationing there — is that once you enter the property, nudity is compulsory.

Do not get me wrong, one of the reasons I love to play golf is to commune with nature, but wearing nothing but my birthday suit as I walk from tee to green is not my style. But as the French say, *à chacun son goût*. This translates as "to each their taste." Who am I to judge?

Still, I'll leave it to the French and the nudists of the world to let it all hang out and feel the Atlantic Ocean breezes tickle their privates as they amble naked down the fairway. Oh, and if you ever find yourself at La Jenny, there is one other mandatory requirement beyond baring it all: you must take a shower before arriving at the first tee!

DANGER, DANGER ...

It's not much of a course (it only features one hole), but it is definitely the world's most dangerous. Located in the border town of Panmunjom, just a chip shot from the demilitarized zone that divides North and South Korea, Camp Bonifas (formerly Camp Kitty Hawk) features a fairway lined by barbed wire and dotted with trenches. The 192-yard-long, par 3 one-hole "golf course" lies inside the military garrison guarded by United States and South Korean troops.

The course was originally built to offer soldiers stationed there some recreation. Beware as you walk from the tee to the green (made of AstroTurf): the hole is surrounded on all three sides by active minefields. Over the years, more than one errant shot has set off a landmine.

No wonder the following sign welcomes visitors — and warns first-time players of the inherent risks of teeing it up at Camp Bonifas: "Danger, never take the ball from an active landmine hole!"

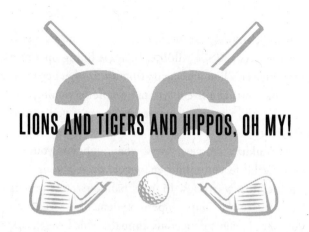

LIONS AND TIGERS AND HIPPOS, OH MY!

Most golfers enjoy spotting wildlife on the course. Usually, sightings are limited to animals that are wary of the players and animals that pose little or no threat. Sure, in certain regions of North America, golfers encounter snakes and alligators. Bears sometimes amble around Rocky Mountain courses and kangaroos are common in Australia. But you have not had a real animal experience until you play Skukuza, where predators prowling the fairways are, pardon the pun, par for the course.

Dubbed the "wildest course on Earth," Skukuza Golf Club is located adjacent to Kruger National Park — South Africa's largest wildlife sanctuary. The park features more species of large mammals than any other African game reserve, including the "big five" (lions, leopards, rhinoceroses, elephants, and African buffaloes). There is no barrier between golfers and the wildlife. Imagine lining up a birdie putt with a lazy lion looking on from the bushes beyond the green or spotting a five-metre-tall giraffe munching leaves off a tree and peering down at you to see if you read the putt right.

At Skukuza, you never know what might join your foursome. Wildlife you might encounter during your round also includes warthogs, hippos, baboons, and impalas. According to the course superintendent, the African buffaloes are the most dangerous animals, which weigh up to nine hundred kilos and are equipped with a pair of large horns. Their movements and actions are unpredictable.

How did this untamed terrain inside a national park become a golf course? Passion and politics. After the Second World War, a fund was created for recreational and sporting activities for the staff at Kruger Park. First, a rugby and cricket field was created; then, a few years later, a pair of golf lovers — Nic de Beer and Jan Viljoen — who had been playing near the park decided that land, which at the time was being used for a rugby field, had potential for some holes. Their dream was realized when they, along with a few other golf enthusiasts, persuaded a farmer who owned land adjacent to Kruger National Park to cede them some of his property to build a course. On June 12, 1971, six players teed off on the forerunner to the Skukuza Golf Club

(Toulon Golf Club), and by 1974, Skukuza was completed for the exclusive use and enjoyment of Kruger Park staff.

In 1999 the nine-hole course opened to the general public. Before teeing off, golfers must sign an "activity indemnity form." To limit risks to golfers, the greenskeeper and the turf and maintenance crew tour the course before dawn each morning to scout for any dangerous predators getting too close. If they find any, they'll deem the course temporarily unsafe and close a few holes until they can get the predators to move. To illustrate: one early morning in August 2022, the turf crew found a slain giraffe sprawled across the third fairway — a situation that led to a feeding frenzy involving lions and hyenas.

While playing golf at Skukuza poses more risks than most courses, there have been few attacks reported in the fifty years of its existence. The only reported death occurred in 2014, when Jacques van der Sandt went waist-deep into Lake Panic (the body of water that lies between the tee and green on the course's signature ninth hole) to retrieve golf balls and became dinner for a crocodile.

THE WORLD'S MOST EXTREME 19TH HOLE

In golf, the nineteenth hole is slang for the barroom in the clubhouse. The term first appeared in print in an 1890 article published in Dundee, Scotland's *Evening Telegraph*. Today, before reaching this post-round drink spot, many courses offer an actual nineteenth hole as a fun bonus for golfers to cap their round. No extra hole is as spectacular or breathtaking as the "Extreme 19th" at South Africa's Legend Golf & Safari Resort — located a two-and-a-half-hour drive from Johannesburg, close to the Zimbabwe border. Have a fear of heights? Just reading about this terrifying hole might put you over the edge.

Included in the green fee is a helicopter trip to a tee that sits on a cliff on Hanglip Mountain, 484 metres above sea level. The green, shaped like the African continent, is 395 yards away and 434 yards below where you tee off! The course claims the hole is the world's longest and also highest par 3. The average hang time for tee shots is twenty-two seconds. To help golfers locate balls that miss the green, the club employs caddies who are equipped with crash helmets.

The idea of building the hole came to Legend Holdings CEO Peet Cilliers after taking part in a family picnic at the summit of Hangklip Mountain. When he returned later with a friend to marvel at this view and share a bottle of wine, the two hatched the harebrained idea — they thought it would add some extra excitement to anyone's visit. South African golf legend Gary Player (nine-time major champion) struck the ceremonial first tee shot on the Extreme 19th in 2008. As a gimmick and as a way to draw tourists in its inaugural year, a $1 million prize was offered to anyone who managed to ace the hole. Luckily for the resort, no one made a hole-in-one.

When the Legend Golf & Safari Resort opened its signature eighteen holes several months after the Extreme 19th was inaugurated, it also gave golfers a unique experience: the chance to play the longest course in South Africa, a course where each of the holes was designed by a different professional golfer, who together hail from sixteen different countries. The resort also includes a ten-hole, par 3 tribute course — each hole is a nod to a famous par 3 from around the globe.

Playing the 19th is optional, but your green fee at the Legend's signature course includes the helicopter ride to the hole, up to seven shots off the tee depending on wind conditions, a DVD, and a souvenir hat to commemorate this terrifying bucket-list experience.

The savannah swallows more balls than ever reach the green, and only fourteen people have ever birdied the Extreme 19th. Morgan Freeman once parred the hole. Phil Collins made a double bogey. An electric fence surrounds the green to keep the most dangerous predators at bay. The cost? Not that extreme: five thousand rand ($263) for a foursome to play just the 19th and $52 to play the Legend's signature course. It is hard to believe, but some thrill seekers travel halfway around the world just to play this one-of-a-kind hole.

NO GREEN IS AN ISLAND, OR IS IT?

Ready to whet your appetite? Creativity is stamped all over the history of golf course design. With a blank canvas at their disposal, architects use the land and their limitless imaginations to dream up layouts that both challenge and delight players. Sometimes a design will make golfers wonder just what the course's creator was thinking.

Probably no design makes players give their heads a few nervous shakes before teeing off more than the famed seventeenth hole at TPC Sawgrass. The par 3 in Ponte Vedra Beach, Florida, is not long. A pitching wedge is usually all that's needed to reach the green, located just under 137 yards from the tee. What's the catch? The green is actually an island that measures sixty-eight feet from front to back and eighty-one feet from side to side. No postage stamp, but still a tough target. Add in frequent trade winds and it's no wonder even the world's best golfers — who play the hole as part of the PGA Tour's Players Championship each year — are befuddled over this short shot.

Just how difficult is this hole? Since the inaugural Players Championship in 2003, 990 balls have been dunked by the world's best. During the 2023 tournament alone, the pros sank fifty-eight balls into this lake. According to the club, on average, over the course of thirty-five thousand rounds played annually, about sixty thousand balls are hit into the water. That's more than one million balls lost to this lake over just twenty-two years! Four times a year, divers enter these waters and risk getting nipped by an alligator to retrieve the thousands of balls lost.

If you ever play this infamous hole, go ahead and hit as many balls as you want, but there is an unwritten local rule to help speed play (and also reduce embarrassment): if you shoot three shots into the drink, it's time to lift your head, pick up your ball, and play on.

This revolutionary par 3 is not the product of design; the creation of its innovative island green was an accident. When American golf course architect Pete Dye designed the course, the hole was supposed to be a simple par 3 with a man-made lake to cross. But as the small pond near the green was excavated to extract sand and material to use elsewhere in shaping the course, water flowed from the pond and most of the putting surface was surrounded by water. Pete credits his wife and design partner, Alice, with the improvised island green idea to solve this problem.

Since the Dyes unveiled their devilish design, hundreds of imitators have mimicked the idea they pioneered. These tricked up, sometimes gimmicky holes have usually become marketing tools for courses to promote their destination. In Florida alone, there are eighteen other island greens.

Here are three other famous island greens:

- Apple Tree. You guessed it, the green at this course in Yakima, Washington, is shaped like an apple, a tribute to the century-old apple orchard that formerly stood on this eighteen-hole course. At 180 yards, this par 3 is a fun challenge that golfers travel from far and wide to play. Players get to this fruit-shaped green via a narrow bridge that resembles the apple's stem.

- Coeur d'Alene Resort in Idaho. This Pacific Northwest course features a bucket-list experience: a green that floats and can be moved to change the yardage. This unique feat of engineering opened in 1991 and plays anywhere from ninety to 220 yards. The 2,200-ton floating green is moved via an underwater cable system. Players are ferried to the putting surface by boat.

- Punta Mita in Mexico at the Four Seasons Hotel. The third hole on the resort's Pacifico Course claims that it is the world's only natural island green. A rock juts out of the ocean upon which a green was built. You can only play this hole, labelled 3B, at low tide. An alternative hole is available at high tide. A sign adjacent to the tee alerts players to whether or not this island green is open or not each day.

TEE TIME

The original thirteen rules of golf, published in 1744, include one that requires players to tee balls off the ground. For the first hundred years, golfers literally sculpted these "tees" from wet sand placed at the start of each hole to make a natural mound for the ball to sit upon.

A pair of Scots are credited with the creation of the first reusable tee. First made with cork and rubber, these tees were used for decades before wooden tees became the norm. In 1889 William Bloxsom and Arthur Douglas were granted a patent for their invention: a small rubber plate with a raised support, which resembled a pair of upright prongs, for a golf ball to sit on. This first tee balanced above the ground rather than being pushed into the earth, as future iterations were, which made getting the tee to stick and hold the ball — especially on windy days — difficult.

The first tee that kept the ball still, even when the winds whipped, was the "Perfectum." In 1892 Percy Ellis of Surrey, England, patented an improved tee that had an iron spike as its base. Tweaks to the tee continued to be made, each change helping to make this simple piece of golf equipment ever more functional. Today, plastic tees are the preferred choice of golfers, since they do not break too often; but in an age of eco-conscious consumers, biodegradable wooden tees are back in golfers' bags.

The design that led to the eventual mass marketing of tees in North America is attributed to a pair of dentists. In 1899 Dr. George Grant, frustrated by having to use the sand mounds located at each hole to create tees for his balls, designed a concave peg golfers could easily push into the ground. The result was U.S. patent No. 638,920: the first wooden golf tee.

Grant never had the means to mass-market his product, however. It was not until the 1920s when Dr. William Lowell from New Jersey — another dentist — patented what he called the "Reddy Tee." This hollowed-out wooden peg was just a simple evolution of Grant's idea. Due to his marketing genius — he enlisted one of the greatest golfers of that era, Walter Hagen, to promote his invention by using it at all his exhibition matches and leaving behind samples everywhere he played — his invention became enormously popular, leading to six figure sales as early as 1922 and forever changing the game.

TAMING A TIGER

Everything about Eldrick "Tiger" Woods's golf story is fascinating, so how does one pick one tale about the greatest golfer to ever play the game? You do not. Instead, you try to catch this Tiger by the tail by capturing just a few highlights.

By the age of two, Woods was already hitting a golf ball with a sawed off, shortened golf club that his dad (Earl) made for him. He made his debut on TV on *The Mike Douglas Show* that same year when he and his father were invited to be guests after Douglas saw a news clip of Tiger hitting golf balls at a local driving range. Arriving on set carrying a small bag with a few clubs on his back, the toddler wowed the host, the studio audience, and the other two guests that night (comedian Bob Hope and actor Jimmy

Stewart) by hitting a golf ball with the skill of someone six or seven times his age.

By age three, Tiger was shooting 45 for nine holes. He broke 80 for eighteen holes by the time he was eight, and at twelve broke 70 for the first time. Tiger is tied with Sam Snead for the most professional wins: eighty-two. Next to Jack Nicklaus, who has eighteen, Woods has also won the most Majors of any professional golfer (fifteen).

In 1997, when he was only twenty-one, he won his first Masters, becoming the first non-white person to win a green jacket. He did it by lapping the rest of the field — winning by twelve strokes. Tiger set a pair of records in that tournament: the youngest to win and the largest margin of victory. That is a record that's unlikely to be beat. Twenty-two years later, at forty-three, Tiger won his fifth Masters trophy. This is regarded as one of the greatest comebacks in sports history as, age aside, the win came following years of personal off-course issues and injuries that included four back surgeries. Even Woods believed he might never golf again, let alone win.

In his prime, Tiger dominated the sport and fuelled its growth, both at the professional and grassroots level. He held the world number one ranking for 683 weeks, including a stretch of 281 consecutive weeks, and between 1998 and 2005 he made the cut in 142 consecutive events.

No one has ever managed to achieve the modern Grand Slam — winning the four major championships all in one year — but Woods came the closest, winning the 2000 U.S. Open, British Open, and PGA Championship, and then winning the Masters in 2001. He held all four trophies at the same time. For his feat, a new term was coined: the Tiger Slam.

THIS IS HOW WE ROLL

Early golf was typified by uneven lies and rolling fairways and greens not meant to play fast. In the nineteenth century, workers cut golf course greens with a scythe, leaving the grass the same height as what is common today on fairways and tees. So, how did these maintenance practices evolve from a standard mowing height of 1.5 centimetres for a green to the mowing height many of the top private golf courses trim their greens to today (0.5 centimetres) … almost killing the turf by scalping it this low for most major championships? The answer: technological advances combined with golfers' demands for slicker surfaces.

Englishman Edwin Budding invented the first mechanized reel mower, receiving a patent for his device in 1830. Budding's machine did not arrive in the United States until four decades later. Initially, this mower was horse-drawn and used mainly by farmers. It took some time, however, before the mower was finally adopted by those charged with keeping golf courses in shape. By the 1920s, specialized greens mowers were creating greens cut tighter than your standard military haircut.

Industry-leading brand Toro developed the first roller-type greens mower in 1923; it was built specifically to cut creeping bentgrass — the preferred kind of turfgrass used to seed greens in that era. It could also handle Bermuda grasses, which were popular in southern climes. According to the company, by 1940, more than 80 percent of all eighteen-hole courses in the United States used the firm's manual putting greens mower. It was the industry standard until powered mowers arrived. An interesting aside: in 1928 Toro developed the first all-electric powered greens mower, but it did not catch on.

•

With improvements in design, greens mowers became able to cut grass shorter and shorter. As the length of the grass on putting greens decreased, the speed of the surface increased. While this made golfers happy, there remained the issue of inconsistency in the speeds of putting surfaces from course to course. Golfers liked fast greens, but they also wanted consistency. PGA Tour players, in particular, complained about this. They would get used to the speed of the greens on a given course one week only to be dumbfounded by the difference in the greens at the next tournament.

A famous example of the problem caused by inconsistent green speeds involved Gene Sarazen. He misread the speed of the green at the 1936 U.S. Open at Oakmont Country Club and putted a ball off the green and into the bunker. Reading about this maddening inconsistency prompted Edward S. Stimpson, a Massachusetts state amateur champion and captain of the Harvard golf team, to set out to find a way to measure green speeds.

Stimpson produced his first prototype in 1936; he used this tool to take measurements at a sampling of golf clubs and continued this research for the next three and a half decades. It was not until 1978 that the United States Golf Association adopted the golfer's invention and made it the official tool to measure green speeds.

Known today as the Stimpmeter, this simple tool, which is basically a ninety-centimetre-long, sixty-centimetre-wide ramp, is the standard way superintendents measure green speed. How does the Stimpmeter work? Golf balls are placed in a notch at the top of this ramp and slowly it is raised to a twenty-degree angle. Then, the balls are allowed to roll down the ramp and run out on the flattest section of the green being tested. The process is repeated from where these balls landed to make sure the reading is consistent in both directions. The number of feet the ball rolls from the top of the ramp is its Stimp rating, or what today golfers call a green's speed.

When the Stimpmeter was first introduced in 1978, the average green speed was about 6.5. Today, most PGA Tour events have green speeds around twelve, while most public courses are less than nine. Modern greenskeepers use a number of different practices to ensure that the desired green speed is achieved: lightweight rolling is employed several times a week and the grass is mowed at two- to three-day intervals, each mow lowering the height of the grass gradually, by 0.13-millimetre increments.

32

A COLOMBIAN COURSE
CRAFTED OUT OF SPITE

Have you ever shown up late for your tee time and had the starter say, "Sorry, we are fully booked, please come back tomorrow"? What's your reaction? Do you throw a tantrum? Or do you go have a coffee with your foursome instead?

Well, imagine having so much money that, instead, out of spite, you react to this slight by building your own course. A golfer in Colombia did just this. I learned his story, and many other fascinating stories, from my caddie while golfing in Colombia, where I sampled some of this South American country's finest *campos de golf.*

Ruitoque Golf & Country Club in Bucaramanga was definitely the highlight of my tour. Some courses amaze you with their design, some with their views, some with their overall ambience. Ruitoque had it all. In particular, the vistas of the surrounding green Andes were astonishing, unlike anything I've ever seen while golfing. This Jack Nicklaus–designed course (the first he created in the country) in the province of Santander is the most spectacular *campo de golf* I've ever played.

According to the story of its creation, a well-heeled developer, who was a member of Club Campestre de Bucaramanga, the only other club in the area, showed up late for his tee time for the annual club championship and was refused entry into the tournament. So, to spite the club, he built a rival course, featuring it in an exclusive condominium development located up a winding mountain road.

The Ruitoque 1,250-acre gated community features its own grocery store, spa, and many other amenities — including a golf course. As if building a rival course wasn't a big enough way of flipping the bird to his former club, to add that extra sprinkle of salt to the wound he hired one of the greatest-ever golfers to design an eighteen-hole championship golf course. Ruitoque is filled with many classic Nicklaus design traits — from large fairway bunkers to challenging pin placements. The private course, which opened in 1997, is a 6,600-yard par 71.

The story behind Ruitoque's creation is just one of the many fascinating tales you'll discover golfing in Colombia.

The country has more than fifty golf courses, many of which are considered the best in all of Latin America. Famed North American designers past and present — from the aforementioned Nicklaus to Canada's own Stanley Thompson and American Robert Trent Jones — have all left their marks on Colombia's *campos de golf.*

33 GOING FOR GOLD

David vs Goliath. The United States vs Canada.
This is the story of how a forty-six-year-old Toronto insurance salesman who suffered from diabetes defeated a heavily favoured American — twenty-six years his junior — to win the first-ever Olympic gold medal in golf.

One of thirteen children, George S. Lyon needed to find some way to stand out among all his siblings. Sports were one area where he excelled. At eighteen, he set a Canadian record in the pole vault. He was also a talented baseball and cricket player. Although he would become the first winner an Olympic gold for the sport, surprisingly, Lyon did not play golf until he was thirty-eight years old. A natural talent from the first day he picked up a golf club, this self-taught man, approaching middle age, won the Canadian Amateur only eighteen months after playing his first round. He went on to win the event another seven times. Not satisfied with his home-grown trophies, Lyon dreamed bigger, and early in the twentieth century, his Olympic dreams came true.

In 1904, in St. Louis, golf was an official Olympic sport — for only the second time.* Lyon travelled the 1,200 kilometres by train from Toronto to St. Louis, which also happened to be hosting the World's Fair that year. There he and two of his countrymen competed against seventy-two Americans. For a number of reasons, mostly due to cost and a last-minute move of the Games from Chicago, all the top golfers from the United Kingdom had taken a pass on travelling to St. Louis.

The tournament was held at Glen Echo Country Club. After easily winning his first three matches, Lyon met Chandler Egan in a thirty-six-hole final. Lyon apparently drove the green on the opening 276-yard par 4, and that set the tone. The twenty-year-old Chandler, the reigning U.S. Amateur champion, had arrived at Glen Echo as the gold medal favourite. He was definitely shaken, and Lyon ended up shocking the young American and the media with a three-and-two win. What made Lyon's golden victory even more incredible is that it was his first time competing in a tournament in the United States.

---

* Golf was part of the 1900 Olympics in Paris, France. American Charles Sands won the event, but no medals were awarded.

For 112 years, George S. Lyon was the correct answer to this difficult trivia question: "Who was the last golfer to win an Olympic gold medal?" The sport did not return to the Games until 2016 in Rio de Janeiro, Brazil, when England's Justin Rose stood atop the podium.

Lyon travelled to London for the 1908 Olympic Games to defend his title, but a disagreement over the format led to all U.K. competitors withdrawing and the cancelling of the event. Lyon, as the lone player left, was offered the gold medal as a consolation, but he declined.

A final tidbit to share, which makes Lyon's story even more fascinating: his gold medal is nowhere to be found. Somehow, along the way, it got lost. Or did it? It's a mystery that no one — not his family nor the Canadian Golf Hall of Fame curators — have yet solved. The sterling silver trophy he received for that Olympic triumph in St. Louis is still around and is in safekeeping at the Hall of Fame, but not that mysterious medal. Maybe one day it will be found in a secret hiding spot, or maybe Lyon melted it down to pay for some of life's pleasures. Regardless of whether or not the medal ever resurfaces, this golden golf story is entrenched in Canadian sports history.

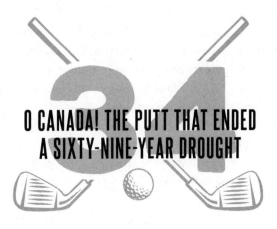

O CANADA! THE PUTT THAT ENDED A SIXTY-NINE-YEAR DROUGHT

June 11, 2023, is a date Canadian golf fans will remember forever. Where Canadians were when "the putt" was taken will be remembered just as Americans remember the famous February day in 1980 when the "Miracle on Ice" occurred.[*]

On that early spring evening, at Toronto's Oakdale Golf & Country Club, Canadian golfer Nick Taylor made golf history. The PGA Tour player ended a sixty-nine-year drought for Canada by winning the RBC Canadian Open. Before Taylor, Pat Fletcher was the last Canadian male to win the Open — and that was way back in 1954. The

---

[*] The "Miracle on Ice" occurred February 22, 1980, in Lake Placid, New York, when the U.S.A. hockey team upset the Soviet Union to win the gold medal at the Winter Olympics.

thirty-five-year-old native of Abbotsford, British Columbia, not only lifted this monkey off the backs of all his fellow Canadian golfers, but he took the trophy from Englishman Tommy Fleetwood in dramatic fashion — sinking a seventy-two-foot putt for eagle on the fourth playoff hole. The putt was the longest Taylor had ever made in his PGA Tour career. *Golfweek* named the epic stroke the Shot of the Year. As the ball trickled into the hole, CBS Sports commentator Jim Nantz, in a nod to the opening lines of Canada's national anthem, said, "Glorious and free."

Stunned by his glorious shot, Taylor flipped his TaylorMade Spider Tour Red putter in the air and leapt into his caddie's arms. Pandemonium followed. Players and fans rushed the green, creating a scene more akin to the end of a U.S. college basketball game. Adding to the lore of this historic day was a tackle, something more likely to occur on the gridiron than on a golf green. Taylor's fellow Canadian — PGA Tour player Adam Hadwin — ran toward his friend spraying champagne from a bottle only to be thrown to the ground by a security guard just doing their job.

Before sinking that improbable shot, Taylor made many clutch putts to stay in contention. After shooting a three-over par 75 in the opening round, he was in danger of not making the cut. However, Taylor followed up with a round of 67 on Friday and a course-record nine-under

63 on Saturday. He needed to make an eleven-footer for a birdie on the seventy-second hole to shoot a final round 66 to force the playoff.

How iconic was this win for Canada and for golf within the country? "The Putt" is now part of a reimagined logo for the RBC Canadian Open. Taylor's putter drop image is now the "I" in Canadian — it replaces an old part of the tournament brand that featured an old-school golfer sporting a newsboy cap.

A PAIR OF DOUBLE-DOUBLES

Canadians are known for their love of double-doubles from Tim Hortons, hot coffee with two packs of sugar and two shots of cream. Back in 1985, at the U.S. Open held at Oakland Hills Country Club, just outside Detroit, Taiwanese golfer Chen Tze-Chung (T.C. Chen) served up not just one, but a pair of double-doubles on the golf course. His had nothing to do with coffee, but each was similar — one was pretty sweet, the other was scalding.

First the good, then the ugly. In the first round, Chen, the first Chinese golfer to earn a PGA Tour card, holed a 3-wood from 256 yards on the par 5 for double eagle to put him in the lead after the first eighteen holes of this major competition. His 65 tied the course record. Chen followed with a pair of 69s that kept him on top heading into the final round.

He ran into trouble on the fourth hole on Sunday, however. His third shot on this par 4 found the thick rough just short of the green. Taking a wedge, he swung with all his might. Unfortunately, the club got caught briefly in the grass causing the dreaded "double-double" — his club hit the ball twice, which according to the *Rules of Golf* results in a one-stroke penalty (players are not allowed to hit a ball that is still in motion). When Chen finally tapped in to make a quadruple bogey (a four-over 8 on the par 4 or as this score is referred to by golfers, "a snowman"), his four-shot lead was gone. He was livid and never recovered, though Chen did finish in a tie for second place.

Since that fateful shot, anytime a golfer double hits the ball, their playing partners will holler that they just pulled a "T.C. Chen!" Though it does not help him now, anyone who has ever had one of these embarrassing double-doubles rejoiced when, in 2019, the United States Golf Association and the R&A changed the rule so a double hit is no longer considered a penalty.

36 PRESIDENTIAL PASTIMES

At least a dozen of the forty-six men who have served as U.S. president have had a passion for golf that some might say was as deep as their love for politics. Some played the game for leisure, others as a way to relieve stress. And many played the game for political purposes — a round offered the perfect opportunity to negotiate deals.

William Howard Taft was the first president addicted to golf. He played so much during the 1908 presidential campaign that his predecessor, Theodore Roosevelt, urged Taft to quit the game. Woodrow Wilson was perhaps the most golf-mad White House resident. The twenty-eighth U.S. president's fervour for the game was so extreme that he had his Secret Service agents paint his golf balls black so he could play in the snow in winter!

During his eight-year presidential term, he played more than 1,200 rounds.

After Wilson, Dwight D. "Ike" Eisenhower was the most avid golfer to occupy the Oval Office. It's reported Ike played more than eight hundred rounds of golf during his eight-year tenure. Prior to becoming commander-in-chief, Eisenhower was invited to Augusta National by co-founder Cliff Roberts. The pair formed a fast friendship, and he became a member of the private club. Eisenhower made forty-five trips there in his lifetime (twenty-nine during his presidency). Roberts had a house constructed on the grounds (now known as the Eisenhower Cabin) for Ike and his wife, Mamie, to stay in during their visits.

A twenty-metre loblolly pine that guarded the left side of the fairway on Augusta's seventeenth was later named the Eisenhower Tree. This was a bit of an inside joke — Ike had unsuccessfully lobbied to have the tree removed, since he considered it a menace, ruining the hole. In 2014, following damage during an ice storm, more than forty-five years after his death, this tall tree was finally cut down.

The home of the Masters has an interesting connection with another American leader. On October 22, 1983, Ronald Reagan was playing at Augusta National when a gunman (Charles Harris) crashed his truck through a locked gate and took two hostages in the club's pro shop demanding to speak to the fortieth U.S. president. Fortunately, this incident ended with no injuries when Harris surrendered after a couple of hours.

President Eisenhower hit balls on the White House lawn every day at 5:00 p.m., had a pair of par 3 holes constructed at Camp David (the 125-acre presidential retreat in Maryland), and installed a putting green on the White House lawn. Richard Nixon, out of spite perhaps, had the green removed during his presidency, but another golf-nut president (George H.W. Bush) reinstalled this presidential practice green in 1991. The two-thousand-square-foot green remains, giving future U.S. heads of state the perfect spot to practise their putting.

John F. Kennedy, who enjoyed the game, was a member of Harvard's golf team and played often at D.C.'s Burning Tree Club. He chided his predecessor (Eisenhower) about this obsession, calling him the "Duffer in Chief."

Lyndon B. Johnson may have played the game, but it seems that he was not a very good golfer. According to one historian, the president often took up to four hundred swings during an eighteen-hole round and was known to bend the rules in his favour — hitting balls until he was satisfied with the result. LBJ also used golf as a way to spend time with senators and used these uninterrupted hours to negotiate bills he was looking to get passed, such as the Civil Rights Act of 1964.

Nixon, Eisenhower's vice-president before winning the top post himself, became addicted to the game. Golf has an interesting connection with the Watergate scandal. Nixon's successor — Gerald Ford — after announcing his pardon of Nixon escaped the real world and the criticism of his decision by playing a round of golf with the Big Three (Jack Nicklaus, Arnold Palmer, and Gary Player) as part of the opening of the World Golf Hall of Fame ceremonies in St. Augustine, Florida.

This pastime continues to be popular with U.S. presidents. It figured as part of the first televised debate between 2024 presidential candidates, incumbent Joe Biden and former president Donald Trump, when Trump challenged the forty-sixth president of the United States to a golf match. Trump made no mention of challenging Kamala Harris, Biden's successor as Democratic candidate for president, to a game of golf.

A GOLF TRADITION UNLIKE ANY OTHER

The Masters, in the phrase coined by sports com-
mentator Jim Nantz, is a "tradition unlike any other." As
someone who has been lucky enough to walk the hallowed
golf grounds in Augusta, Georgia, I can attest to how special the course is — and how special the tournament is.

The first golf major each year, the Masters is a tournament of firsts — it was the first to provide complimentary
parking for patrons, it was the first tournament to have
bleachers for fans, and it was first golf tournament to be
broadcast live from coast to coast on the radio.

No other golf club or professional tournament has had
as many books written about it (at least eight). It's also one
of the toughest tickets (or badges as entry passes are called
at the Masters) to snag in all of professional sports.

How were the Augusta National Golf Club and the Masters born? They were the brainchild of Cliff Roberts and Robert Tyre "Bobby" Jones. The course opened in 1932, and the first Masters was played in March 1934. Jones and Roberts's idea was to hold an annual tournament as a way to offer a service to the golf industry by letting non-members enjoy their course. For the first five years, the event was called the Augusta National Invitation Tournament. This feature — only those with the best records are invited to play — is what makes the tournament so prestigious.

Every year, since 2012, the club holds an online lottery for a chance to become a patron and score a badge. Your odds of securing a badge this way are 0.55 percent! Officially, the tournament is "sold out" annually, but there is always an entry to be had if you are willing to pay the price. Once inside, the concessions are cheap: peanuts and pimiento cheese sandwiches are available for munching, and $5 draft beers can be had, served in a souvenir green plastic cup.

The course is constructed on 365-acre piece of land — bought by Clifford Roberts and Bobby Jones for $70,000 — that was formerly Fruitland Nursery. Dr. Alister MacKenzie, a former army surgeon from West Yorkshire, designed the course. Designing golf courses was a hobby for the doctor — until he won a *Country Life* competition to design a golf hole in the United States. This boosted his profile and led to a successful career as a golf course architect.

Over the course of his career, he went on to design golf courses on four continents.

A collection of short fascinating facts about Augusta ... and the Masters:

- Horton Smith, the first winner, received a cheque for $1,500.
- In 1975 Lee Elder became the first black golfer to compete in the Masters.
- The Par 3 contest — played on Augusta's par-3 course — was first played in 1960, with Sam Snead winning the event. It has been a Wednesday tradition at the Masters ever since. Past tournament participants and non-competing past champions are invited to play in this fun event, the day before official action begins.
- A Green Jacket is given out to the champion. It was awarded for the first time in 1949 when Sam Snead won the tournament. The Green Jacket winners receive theirs to keep for twelve months. They must return it to the club for safekeeping afterward, but they can wear it whenever they visit the course.
- In 1952 Walter Hagen hosted a dinner that has become a tradition. Each year since then,

the previous year's winner chooses the menu for the Champions Dinner, held on the night before the tournament begins. Only previous winners and their guests can attend.

THE "OLDEN BEAR"

A Sunday surge. One for the ages and one that gave the middle finger to the ageists. Jack Nicklaus, already enshrined in the history of professional golf as one the game's greatest, gave fans one more golden moment. This is the tale of the improbable. A story of an April in Augusta that even Jack himself, who had admitted he was in the "December of his career," thought was unlikely. This is the story of when he won the 1986 Masters.

Against all odds and competing against players an average of fifteen years younger, Nicklaus somehow came from four shots back to win his sixth Green Jacket at forty-six. In doing so, he became the oldest golfer to ever to win the Masters. For many golf fans, this feat remains their favourite golf memory. It certainly is one of

Nicklaus's, and it was made even more special having his son as his caddie.

Nicklaus was surely inspired by critics like the *Atlanta-Journal Constitution* reporter who in a pre-tournament column called him "washed up." The journalist even poked fun at Jack's nickname, dubbing him "the Olden Bear." That scribe was made to eat his words, but it must be admitted that he was not out of place in his critiques — in the seven PGA Tour events before the Masters that year, Nicklaus had missed the cut three times and withdrawn once.

Starting in the final round, the Golden Bear's name was not even on the first page of the leaderboard. No one gave him a chance. Then, after a birdie on the ninth hole, something clicked, and Nicklaus found another gear. What ensued was one of best back-nine scores in Masters history. He played holes thirteen through seventeen alone in five under par. After draining a long putt to take the lead on the penultimate hole, Nicklaus thrust his putter in the air. A famed photo of this now adorns country clubs across North America. Jack finished with a six-under 30, which included an eagle on fifteen, to post a score only a few players since have surpassed (29 is the current record).

On route to this historic comeback, Nicklaus's tee shot on the par 3 sixteenth was one of the greatest shots ever; he nearly made an ace, hitting his shot to within three feet of the hole. Following up, he made the short putt for yet another birdie. And, on the seventy-second hole, Nicklaus nearly drained a fifty-foot putt, but he made the short tap-in for par to post a final round 65 — giving him the club-house lead — which was just good enough. Neither of the two golfers playing behind him were able to match his total. Greg Norman, who started the day with the lead, ended up tied for second, one shot back, with Tom Kite.

While he did not play in many PGA Tour tournaments after this win and joined the Senior PGA Tour (later re-named the PGA Tour Champions) in 1990, Nicklaus continued to play in the Masters until he officially retired from competitive golf in 2005. This ageless wonder proved he still had game when in 1998, at the age of fifty-eight, he birdied three of the final four holes to finish in a tie for sixth place.

THE RISE OF GOLF IN SOUTH KOREA

Golf was first introduced to this Asian country dur-ing the colonial era when Japan ruled the nation. The officers of the Japanese army brought their love of this sport to Koreans, and it was soon embraced by the country's upper classes. The popularity of the sport slowly grew during the late nineteenth century and early twentieth century. It increased in popularity thanks to British diplomats stationed there and expats, settled mainly in Seoul and Chemulpo, who worked as merchants, missionaries, and in the service of the Korean government.

Just as Tiger Woods's victory at the 1997 Masters — when he was only twenty-one — sparked kids' interest in golf in the United States, Pak Se-ri's win, as a rookie no less, at the 1988 U.S. Women's Open jump-started interest in the sport in South Korea. The first player from the Korean Republic to win a women's professional major, Pak went on to win twenty-four more times, becoming the youngest player — at twenty-nine years old — to be inducted into the World Golf Hall of Fame. Since Pak's first win, the number of golf courses in the country has more than doubled — there are now more than five hundred in South Korea — and native Koreans have won the U.S. Women's Open ten times.

Pak's success has had an enormous impact on the sport in the Republic of Korea. When she won her first major, she was the only player from her country on the Ladies Professional Golf Association Tour. Today, Korea has thirty-eight players ranked in the top one hundred on the women's tour, and four of those are ranked among the top ten in world golf rankings. Inbee Park is one of these "Se-ri kids" — a reference to Pak's influence on the next golf generation. In 2016 she won the women's first-ever golf gold at the Rio Olympics, adding the medal to her total of seven major golf championships. K.J. Choi was the first Korean-born male to play on the PGA Tour. He has racked up eight wins in his career.

Golf is now entrenched in Korean culture. Playing the game is a symbol of affluence and status, and golfers like Park are considered national heroes.

WILLIE'S CLUB, WILLIE'S RULES

"If You've Got the Money, Honey, I've Got the Time." The title of Lefty Frizell's first number one song, which debuted on the country charts in 1950 and which Willie Nelson covered twenty-six years later, is the motto of Pedernales Golf Club — the nine-hole course owned by the country outlaw.

If you ever find yourself "eight songs away from Austin, Texas," you should definitely take the time to tee up at this snub to the country club. Be forewarned: if you are a stickler for the official rules of golf and care more about your score than having fun, this course is not for you. Willie's course, so Willie's rules. There is no dress code, and if you "never have a bad lie then you never have to tell a bad lie!"

The course opened in 1968 as the Briarcliff Yacht and Golf Club. After a decade, Briarcliff declared bankruptcy. Enter Nelson, who had just released *Stardust*, his Grammy-winning album of pop standards. The songwriter, an avid golfer, used $250,000 of his royalties to purchase the club. Willie renamed the course Pedernales after the Colorado River tributary that meanders through the property. After Willie purchased Pedernales, he quipped, "I've always wanted a golf course where I could set the pars!"

As well as setting the pars and making his own rules, Willie has made the course his own. He built a fifty-four-thousand-square-foot home on the property's highest hill and transformed the original clubhouse into a recording studio. His extended family were encouraged to build homes on the grounds too. Over the years, the Rock & Roll Hall of Fame member has recorded many albums at Pedernales, including *Spirit*, *Rainbow Connection*, and *Pancho & Lefty* with Merle Haggard. Willie's Cut-N-Putt, the nickname for Pedernales Golf Club, refers to this studio. While Willie's engineers finished mixing his latest record, Willie played nine holes before listening to the results.

For thirty-three years, Pedernales was Nelson's private playground for his friends and family; then he decided to transform the course into a daily-fee facility. If you go, do not expect pristine conditions. No food is available. And your group, which can be as big as three foursomes, might include die-hard Willie fans dressed in jeans, sporting a red bandana instead of a ball cap, smoking some herb, and blasting music.

Oh, and about Willie's rules. Since it's his club, the Grammy-winning songwriter set the pars and devised his own set of rules that players must follow:

- When another player is shooting, no player should talk, whistle, hum, clink coins, or pass gas.
- Excessive displays of affection are discouraged. Violators must replace divots and will be penalized five strokes.
- Have the office tell your spouse you are in a conference.
- "Freebies" are not recommended for players with short putts.
- No more than twelve in your foursome.
- Gambling is forbidden, unless, of course, you're stuck or you need a legal deduction for charitable or educational expenses.
- No bikinis, mini-skirts, skimpy see-throughs, or sexually exploitative attire allowed. Except on women.

GOLF'S MISUNDERSTOOD GENIUS

There is no other golfer like Moe Norman. Born Murray Irwin Norman in Kitchener, Ontario, the self-taught golfer possessed one of the best striking abilities — late in life, he admitted to a friend that "the only thing I ever wanted to do was be the best ball striker in the world." Well, he definitely accomplished that goal. He had the best strike ever witnessed in this great game. Tiger Woods's comment about Moe makes clear how extraordinary the golfer's natural swing was: "Moe Norman and Ben Hogan were the only two golfers to 'own their swings.'" Lee Trevino remarked that Moe was the "best ball striker I ever saw come down the pipe. I didn't see them all, but I don't know how anyone could hit the ball better than Moe Norman."

High praise indeed, but well earned. Apparently, as a teenager Tiger Woods studied Moe's swing by looking at microfiche stills at his local public library. Watch YouTube videos to see for yourself Norman's pinpoint accuracy and consistency in action. Talk about robotic. Norman would hit drives on the range for hours, and almost without exception, the balls would fly 250 yards, landing almost on top of one another — literally within feet. He was the poster boy for the ten-thousand-hours-of-practice rule Malcolm Gladwell wrote about — he succeeded because he practised and practised. In Moe's case, however, the number of hours practised were easily five times more than the ten thousand hours Gladwell wrote of. He practised as if possessed. His hands were callused, rough, and blackened from the countless hours spent gripping and swinging a golf club.

Too poor to afford clubs when he was young, Moe practised his swing for two years using only a bent branch. Finally, one of the players he caddied for at Westmount Golf & Country Club sold him an old 5-iron to be paid in 10-cent weekly installments.

Moe would later impress people by hitting balls off Coke bottles and performing a variety of other tricks, but there was much more to Moe than showmanship and theatre. He had a pure golf talent and a natural swing unlike anything seen before or since.

Moe has been described as golf's "misunderstood genius." Many revered him, but he was mocked by just as many. Socially awkward, he was never officially diagnosed, but many suspected that he was on the autism spectrum.

Several books on Moe have been written; film scripts on the life of this mercurial, fascinating golfer have been optioned and expired, and new scripts have been written. One of these days, a biopic on his life and times might find its way to a screen somewhere. Until then, here's the best story on Moe according to his biographer Tim O'Connor.[*]

Sometimes Moe cared more about the applause than the game, and that was one of his downfalls as the following tale illustrates. When he wanted to prove people wrong or make a point, he became hyper-focused and let his game do the talking. His feats amazed people. He was very emotional, though, and that focus sometimes disappeared when the game required poise and patience.

Playing in the 1971 Quebec Open, Moe was ridiculed by the fans with hoots and jeers despite leading the tournament with three to play at Summerlea Golf and Country Club. As he teed off on the sixteenth hole, he smashed a drive long and down the middle, as he had done all day. His friend Gary Slatter, who had been following him outside the ropes, turned to Moe and, tired of saying

---

[*] A summarized version of this story is taken from the first chapter of O'Connor's 1995 book, *The Feeling of Greatness: The Moe Norman Story*.

"Good shot!" for the umpteenth time, said instead, "Well, not bad, Moe."

Moe was furious with his friend. "If you could hit it like that, you'd have lotsa money," he replied. Then, wrapping his arms in a bear hug around Slatter, he flipped him upside down and shook his legs barking all the while: "Ok, let's see how much money you got in your pockets!" Naturally, this act elicited laughs from the gallery.

At the eighteenth tee, Moe was still leading the tournament by a stroke. The hole at the time was a long par 4 — 440 yards down into a valley and back up to a green guarded by a small lake. Moe bombed a drive, and then using a 3-wood, put his ball on the green — the first of the day to reach the hole in regulation. He arrived, expecting applause for this feat, but there was no cheering. He was miffed and mystified. The lack of congratulations consumed Moe, and he ended up four putting to hand the tournament to American Jay Dolan.

The following day, Moe and Slatter were playing in a practice round together for the Canadian Open at Richelieu Valley Golf Club just outside Montreal. As he walked onto the tenth tee — a lengthy 233-yard par 3 — a group of waiting reporters bombarded Moe with questions, gently ribbing him about his work with the flat-stick the day before: "How's the putter today, Moe? Any four putts?"

Norman ignored them and turned to face the tee. His

ire apparent in his stride, he silently grabbed a driver from his bag and smashed the shot toward the green. Before seeing the result, he turned to face the scribes, crossed his arms, and proclaimed, "I'm not putting today." As Moe and the reporters all turned to look toward the green, Slatter was the first to see the ball land inches from the cup and then roll into the hole. "A hole-in-one! He called it in the air!" Slatter cried.

·

A personal note: I grew up working in the backshop of Westmount Golf & Country Club in Kitchener where Moe was an honorary member. I recall seeing this character in the pro shop bouncing a ball on his putter non-stop while muttering quickly to himself. He never once let the ball fall.

THE "CRACK OF SPORTS" SAVES SHOCK-ROCKER'S LIFE

From waking up in a hotel room with yet another hangover — and trying to cure it with a can of beer chased by a bottle of whisky — to chasing a little white ball on a golf course instead. That's a big change. For musician Alice Cooper, golf became his saviour, providing him with an alternative to a rock 'n' roll lifestyle marked by debauchery and drug dependency.

When Cooper was inducted into the Arizona Golf Hall of Fame in 2022, he likened golf to his old bad habits: "If you're going to compare it [golf] to drugs, it would be the crack of sports."

The godfather of shock rock, Alice Cooper wrote the classic rock anthems "I'm Eighteen," "School's Out," and

"No More Mr. Nice Guy." Known for over-the-top stage shows where he wore spidery black makeup and draped boa constrictors around his neck, Cooper was also famous for excess in his personal life. During the 1970s, he started every day with a can of beer; he was a proud member of a drinking club called the Hollywood Vampires that included The Who's drummer, Keith Moon; singer-songwriter Harry Nilsson; and the Beatles' John Lennon. These chums drank heavily every night to see who was the last man standing. Today, Cooper is literally the last man standing of the four. His friends died too young, and he did not want to join them as a result of addiction.

The musician says that, quite literally, golf saved his life. The title of his 2007 memoir even pays homage to this deliverance: *Alice Cooper, Golf Monster: A Rock 'n' Roller's Life and 12 Steps to Becoming a Golf Addict.* When Cooper finally overcame his battle with booze and drugs — putting the plug in the proverbial jug — golf became his new addiction. One day, circa 1982, while killing time before a gig in Phoenix, Arizona, he began searching for a new fixation to replace alcohol, which he had recently given up cold turkey. Cooper headed to a local golf course and signed up for a lesson. Before the pro even offered any tips, the Rock and Roll Hall of Fame member grabbed a 7-iron and hit a shot straight down the middle. From that first swing he was hooked.

For more than four decades of endless touring after that first lesson, he regularly set his alarm for 7:00 a.m. The goal was to play thirty-six holes before sound check — eighteen in the morning and eighteen in the afternoon — to keep his mind off booze. His focus was on hitting the golf ball rather than hitting the bottle.

Cooper often states: "Golf is like rock 'n' roll, I never get tired of playing a power chord … it's in my DNA now."

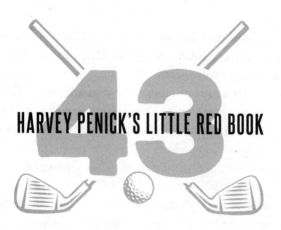

HARVEY PENICK'S LITTLE RED BOOK

A five-by-seven, red Scribbletex notebook, a hum-ble Texas golf instructor, and a journalist named Bud who brought the instructor's scribblings to life. Are these the characters and rough plot for a Hollywood script left in the slush pile? The reality is a story ripe for the big screen. This is the heartwarming tale of how a golf manual ended up becoming required reading for golfers and one of the biggest-selling sports books of all time.

Harvey Penick was born in Austin, Texas. He fell for golf early — he was already earning money as a caddie at Austin Country Club before reaching his double-digit birthday. In 1923, only eighteen years old, Penick became the club's head professional, a position he held until his retirement nearly fifty years later. From 1931 to 1963, Penick also coached the University of Texas golf team — the team won twenty-one NCAA Southwest Conference championships in thirty-three years.

Over the course of a seven-decade career, Penick taught many of the game's greats, including Tom Kite and Ben Crenshaw. Like a philosopher or academic, Penick jotted observations in a notebook — about his pupil's game, tips to remember, and ruminations about all aspects of the game and a life spent teaching it. The golf guru shared this journal with no one but his son. It was always just his "little red book." That changed after a phone call in 1991. That fateful morning, Penick's son Tinsley invited journalist Bud Shrake for a rendezvous with his dad at Austin Country Club.

When Shrake arrived at the club, he spotted Harvey sitting in a golf cart with a briefcase on his lap. He opened the case and handed the journalist a red Scribbletex notebook, telling him no one had read its pages except his son. Shrake spent the rest of that day holed up in one of the cabins on the golf course, poring over Penick's musings. He saw the material's potential, and the idea to turn this journal into a book was hatched.

Putting together a two-page book proposal, Shrake sent it off to Simon & Schuster. The pitch landed on the desk of editor Jeff Neuman, the director of sports books at the publishing house. He knew golf books and saw the sales potential. Neuman gave the proposal the green light and offered an advance of $90,000. Initially, there was some confusion: Penick thought he had to pay the publisher $90,000 and worried how he could afford this. He confessed that he lost some sleep over the issue. Once the miscommunication was cleared up, a contract was signed and the book was published.

Following the 1992 publication of *Harvey Penick's Little Red Book: Lessons and Teachings from a Lifetime in Golf*, neither Shrake nor Penick needed to worry much about money. The book hit number one in the non-fiction category on the *New York Times* bestseller list and has gone on to sell close to one million copies worldwide.

To capture the essence of Penick's original scribblings, the publisher printed the book with a smaller trim size than the standard six-by-nine-inch book. The format became known thereafter in the publishing industry as the "Harvey trim." The book's size wasn't the only thing unique about it. What made the book so different from all the other instruction manuals was Penick's personality, captured perfectly thanks to Shrake's ability to shape Penick's scribbles. His story engaged readers. Using the notebook and the transcripts from hundreds of hours of interviews, Shrake created a work that captured Penick's voice — the book was not just educational, it was also entertaining. Shrake told friends he wanted to create a reading experience that would "be like eating peanuts. You read two or three chapters and you can't stop."

That's the Hollywood-worthy story in a nutshell of how a retired golf pro from Texas became a bestselling author at eighty-seven years old.

WHAT IN THE WORLD: ODDBALL COURSES

What are some of the strangest places a golf course has been built? Try this pair: one in the United States and one in Southeast Asia.

•

Brickyard Crossing: What makes this championship golf course, redesigned by Pete Dye in 1993, so unique is that four of its holes are inside the century-old Indianapolis Motor Speedway, where two of the largest single-day sprint events in the world — the Indianapolis 500 and the Brickyard 400 — are held. Previously called the Speedway 500 Golf Course, it held PGA Tour events annually during the 1960s. Dye incorporated concrete slabs from the racetrack's original walls along the hole's creek beds, and a characteristic of many of Dye's designs — railroad ties — were used to support undulating spectator mounds. The Brickyard Crossing hosted a PGA Champions Tour event from 1994 to 2000 and the Ladies Professional Golf Organization Tour from 2017 to 2019.

•

Merapi Golf Club: This eighteen-hole parkland golf course sits at eight hundred metres above sea level a thirty-minute drive from the ancient city of Yogyakarta, Indonesia, on the island of Java. Developed by local businessman Yuwono Kolopaking in the late 1980s as a gift to the region's people, the course offers panoramic views of Gunung Merapi, or Fire Mountain, the majestic mountain for which it is named. What makes it so special? This "extreme" course is built next to one of the most active and dangerous volcanoes on Earth. Where are you going to take cover when it blows? The last time this happened was 2013, when dust and ash blasted almost a mile into the sky and blanketed this course.

THE ROYAL HOME OF GOLF

How did a field of gorse and heather become a bucket-list stop for global golfers and a tourist destination for non-golfers? Acknowledged today as "the home of golf," the Old Course in St. Andrews, Fife, Scotland, has been enjoyed by golfers since 1400.

Originally, the land upon which the course lies was known as Kilrymont, but the name was changed to honour Saint Andrew, who became the patron saint of Scotland thanks to a Greek monk who, in 357 CE, brought the relics of this apostle to the town. The Old Course dates back to 1552, when a charter granted the townsfolk of St. Andrews use of the public land for golf and other leisure activities. This is the oldest written record of the sport being played on this site, but historians believe people golfed on these grounds for many years before the enactment of this charter.

Today, courses are designed by architects. Millions of dollars are spent to sculpt the landscape to fit these visions. However, the Old Course at St. Andrews, called the Old Lady by some, naturally developed during its first five hundred years. Nothing much was done until Old Tom Morris (considered the game's first ever greenskeeper) created the first green in 1865. The course has 112 bunkers, many of them deep or "pot" bunkers, originally formed by grazing sheep that made these shelters to protect themselves from the wind.

St. Andrews began as a twenty-two-hole course, but the number of holes was later reduced to eighteen. The change came about because in 1764 the Society of St Andrews Golfers, which later became the Royal and Ancient Golf Club (R&A) — the U.K.'s governing body of golf today — decided some of the holes were too short. To correct this, they combined them, reducing the course to eighteen holes. This is the standard number of holes for golf courses built around the world since.

Unsurprisingly, there are a lot of great stories associated with this centuries-old course.

Rabbits play the lead role in one of the best of these. The caretakers of St. Andrews would have welcomed that loveable Looney Tunes character Elmer Fudd, who proclaimed it was "wabbit season" whenever he went on the hunt for Bugs Bunny, during what became known locally as the "rabbit wars." In 1799, strapped for money, the St. Andrews town council sold the links to rabbit breeders. The golfers were furious, as these varmints burrowed and made holes all over the course. The golfers petitioned, like Fudd, to declare hunting season. These "rabbit wars" lasted for sixteen years until a local landowner, who was a golfer, bought the links back and said goodbye for good to these rascally rabbits.

Today, the Old Course (the original links) has hosted the British Open Championship a record twenty-nine times. The home of this golf mecca today includes five other eighteen-hole courses. Collectively, they are known as St. Andrews Links. It is the largest golf complex in all of Europe. The R&A World Golf Museum is also on the property, opposite the clubhouse.

TAKING A GAMBLE ON GOLF

Golf and gambling are a pair of friends as old as the sport. Stories abound of early English kings and dukes wagering on all aspects of this grand old game. Sam Snead, tied, at eighty-two, for the most professional golf wins of all time with Tiger Woods, is quoted as once saying: "I tried to quit gambling once, but it was about as much use as kicking a hog barefoot!"

In the early days of professional golf, players did not receive the exorbitant sums they do today. (Since 2007, PGA Tour players have earned an average of $1 million for putting a golf ball in a hole.) So, to augment their income, they participated in private money matches — side games financed by local hustlers for high stakes.

Back in the day, Tenison Park Golf Course in Dallas,

Texas, was the haven for golf hustlers. This muni (a public course owned by a local municipality) is where one of the game's most infamous hustlers, Titanic Thompson, held court beginning in the early 1930s. Thompson (born Alvin Clarence Thomas) lived to gamble. One of his former wives once told a reporter, "Gambling meant more to him than food, sleep, or love."

Titanic was more than just a gambler; he was a hustler. One of his favourite grifts involved betting that he could drive a golf ball five hundred yards. When a mark took him up on the bet, he led the group to a frozen lake and pounded the ball across the ice.

One of his most famous games was against Byron Nelson — one of the greatest golfers of all time. The "proposition" (his term for bet) was made by three connected gentlemen. They offered to pay Titanic $3,000 to play an eighteen-hole money match against Fort Worth's best golfer. The money match happened at Ridglea, another Texas public course. While it was kept hush-hush — and not covered by the press — it attracted the most notorious gamblers in the Dallas–Fort Worth area, all of whom wanted to get a piece of the action. It became a piece of Lone Star State golf lore later recounted by those that witnessed it. As is true with all such pieces of lore, the details vary depending on who is telling the story. Thompson claimed that he shot 29 on the back nine to beat Nelson and win $3,000. Nelson, on the other hand, always maintained that he was the winner — he declared that the hustler lost despite the fact that he had given him three shots. In the end, Nelson stated that Titanic shot 71 to his 69.

Dick Martin was another of Tenison's famed hustlers. Known as the King, he held court from the 1940s until the 1970s, typically raking in $200 a day from those foolish enough to take a bet. He knew how to spot a mark, knew the course better than most, and regularly took these suckers' money happily. In the process, he became a legend. As one scribe wrote in a 1987 feature in *D Magazine*, aptly titled "The Hustler," "Playing Dick Martin at Tenison Park was like going one-on-one with Larry Bird at Boston Garden. Any way you hooked or sliced it, you had virtually no chance to win."

Modern golfers often enjoy some friendly competition, a.k.a. a wager, with friends. For those with a bigger appetite for betting, there are now many golf-specific gambles — as well as "skins" (a simple game within a foursome where a skin is awarded to the player with the lowest score on each hole) and Nassau bets (basically three bets in one: one for best score on the front nine, one for best back nine, and one for overall score). There are other games, some with funny names — like "bingo bango bongo" (three points given on each hole for the following specific achievements: first on the green [bingo], closest to the pin [bango] and first to hole out [bongo].

Care to make a wager with your friends the next time you tee off? Now, you know the basics of gambling on the golf course and how betting and hustling are intertwined with the sport.

THE DIET COKE-SWILLING GOLF FOLK HERO

Addict (drugs, alcohol, and gambling), Diet Coke– swilling, and chain-smoking John Daly won five tournaments on the PGA Tour (including a pair of golf majors) in a more than thirty-year professional golf career and added several more titles on various other tours on five different continents. Along the way, he destroyed golf courses with his bombs off the tee. Daly also destroyed hotel rooms and marriages. And he made mockeries of some golf holes by putting up big numbers.

The man with the flowing blonde mullet won his first major in 1991 at Crooked Stick in Carmel, Indiana. He initially did not qualify for the tournament; he became the ninth alternate to get in when the other players ahead of him did not take their spots for a variety of reasons. Fate smiled on him, however, and the twenty-five-year-old PGA Tour rookie won, becoming an overnight golf folk hero for the everyman. The tagline on the cover of *Sports Illustrated* proclaimed this unexpected arrival eight days after his incredible victory: "Long Shot: Big Hitter John Daly in a Big PGA Upset."

Daly was at home in Tennessee when Nick Price called to let him know he was withdrawing from the tournament because his wife was about to give birth; this bumped Daly into the first alternate position, allowing him to play. With less than twenty-four hours until the opening round, he jumped into his car and drove the eight hundred kilometres to Crooked Stick, ready to give it the old college try, despite the fact that he'd had no practice and was living on sleep deprivation.

The free-wheeling, blue-collar Daly — who during the tournament stayed at a cheap motel and ate mostly McDonald's — was already turning heads during his inaugural season on the PGA Tour with his mammoth drives. (He led the Tour in driving distance from 1991 to 1993 and also from 1995 to 2002). But as the old saying in the game goes, "Drive for show and putt for dough." The question for the long-ball hitter was, Did he have a complete game to win on the Tour?

In his memoir, *My Life in and out of the Rough*, Daly admits that for years his best friend was Jack Daniel's — he often drank a fifth of a twenty-six-ounce bottle a day in those days.

Daly shot 69 in the first round, three off the lead. The second round was delayed when, the next day, a devastating lightning storm blew through the area — and a golf fan was killed. After that tragic event, the game continued. By the end of round two, in which he shot 67, Daly was eight under par and leading the tournament. To celebrate, Daly high-fived some of the fans outside the ropes, who were delirious with the blond bomber's performance.

Heading to the weekend, Daly started slapping hands and giving guys high-fives on every hole. The crowds swelled as word got around town of what was happening at Crooked Stick. His fans were screaming stuff like, "Kill it, Big John!" On Saturday night, the Indianapolis Colts owner Jim Irsay invited the golfer to the team's NFL game. Reflecting back on this experience, Daly said he felt like the mayor of the city due to the reception he received when he walked out on the field at halftime of that pre-season football game.

On Sunday morning, Daly arrived at Crooked Stick with a three-shot lead over Kenny Knox and Craig Stadler. Waiting for him before he teed off in that final round was an unexpected handwritten note from his childhood hero: "Go get 'em, John," from Jack Nicklaus. Today, this note is kept in a frame at Daly's home.

That inspirational note from one of the game's greatest players certainly helped Daly seal the deal. A heartwarming part of this underdog story not often told involves what Daly did with some of his winnings. Of the $230,000 he won at the 1991 PGA Championship, Daly donated $30,000 to an educational fund for the two daughters of the thirty-nine-year-old man who was struck and killed by lighting. As Daly wrote in his memoir, "It's not like I had a whole lot of money to be giving away back then, but it felt like the right thing to do. I was depressed about the whole thing ... and for some reason felt partly responsible. I said on the spot that if I won the tournament, I would do something for the man's two children."

IT'S ALL ABOUT THE HIPS

Gary Player is a fitness freak. He watches what he eats and exercises religiously — it's reported Player dead-lifted 136 kilos and still did hundreds of sit ups well into his eighties. This lifestyle certainly helped Player on the course.

The South African is considered one of the greatest golf-ers — not just of his generation but of all time. Over the course of his professional career, he recorded more than 150 wins. Not bad for a guy who at the age of fourteen told his father he wasn't interested in giving golf a try because it was "a sissy game." In 1959, at just twenty-three, he won his first British Open championship — the youngest ever to do so. He went on to compete in the tournament a record forty-six consecutive times, winning three Claret Jugs.

A fun fact about that win: in those days, the winner was responsible for commissioning someone to engrave their name on the trophy. When the Claret Jug was returned the following year, the R&A noticed Player's name was etched larger than any of the previous winners!

Two years later, he became the first international player to win the Masters. After winning that Green Jacket, everyone wanted a piece of Player. Calls came from various companies offering sponsorship deals to endorse their products. Following that Masters win, the South African was invited on the *Ed Sullivan Show*. A few days after that national TV appearance, Player's manager received a telegram from the King — Elvis Presley — requesting a meeting with the golfer. Of course, he accepted. In an interview several years ago, Player talked about this experience:

> I walk in there and he's doing a movie called *Blue Hawaii*. As I walk in there, he says, "Cut!" I had a jacket and tie on, and I was going to meet the King. He goes in the room and puts on a jacket, and he comes out with that Southern accent, and he says, "How do you do, sir? I want to play golf."
>
> Well, he had a grip that looked like a cow giving birth to a roll of barbed wire.... So first I get his grip right.

He says, "What else is important?"

I said, "Elvis, you've got to use those hips now. You've got to wind up with the hips and unwind with the hips."

He says, "You're talking to the right man, dear boy."

And Elvis gives that little head a shake and goes zip zip zip zip zip! You know how he moved those hips? Man, could he move those hips!

Then he put his arm around me and said, "Don't step on my blue suede shoes!"

A SILENT, SECRET PLAYGROUND FOR THE RICH AND FAMOUS

Redtail Golf Club, an exclusive golf course in Ontario farm country, is bucket-list worthy, if you are lucky enough to get an invite. (I did once thanks to my friend Lorne Rubenstein, who is an honorary member.) Not only do you need luck getting an invite, you need luck finding it. There is little signage, and there's no grand approach to the club. There are also no lavish gates with security guards. Members figure if you can find it, you had an invitation.

And, speaking of members, the club's membership model is not traditional. When it opened, the owners were only interested in catering to themselves and their inner circle. This initial group of lucky golfers numbered 115. These golfers paid an annual, non-refundable deposit of $1,500, to which their green fees were applied. Any additional rounds had to be paid for individually, along with meals and accommodation. There were no tee times, so you could usually play as many holes as you wanted, when you wanted. An honour system was in place when it came down to what you drank at the bar.

Located just north of Port Stanley, a cottage town on the shores of Lake Erie, the private club is named after the redtail hawks that nest on the property. Designed by English golf course architect Donald Steel, Redtail Golf Club opened in 1992. The feeling of excitement is palpable the moment you step on the property. The greens are slick, the fairways undulating and always in pristine condition.

The course, located on 210 acres, cost $2.2 million to build, but this figure has long been disputed, as many other new courses built during the golf boom of the 1990s and early 2000s could see construction costs exceed $10 million. Regardless, this dream, realized by John Drake and Chris Goodwin, a pair of London, Ontario, businessmen, using profits from the windfall they received from selling their company, Wolverine Tube (a copper pipe manufacturer), is a special place of "privilege and peace."

The club is so special that it has attracted both PGA Tour legends and celebrities alike. During its more than thirty years of existence, it has hosted an array of celebrities from Sean Connery and Michael Douglas to Queen

Elizabeth II, who once stayed in one of the property's cottages. Often, these celebrities jetted in on private planes for just a round. "There is a sense of silence at Redtail," Connery once recalled to Rubenstein, adding, "There is not a place like it anywhere."

THE NUMBER ONE COURSE IN THE WORLD

How did a golf course located in New Jersey be-come perennially ranked by *Golf Digest* and other pundits as the number one course in the world and one of the most exclusive? It's quite the story.

In 1913 George Crump, a Philadelphia hotelier, built the Pine Valley Golf Club on 623 acres of swampland, just beyond the borders of Pennsylvania. The location might not have been a great one, but he was willing to do whatever was necessary to create a great course. It was a pet project, one the golf-obsessed hotelier was happy to spend a fortune on.

In order to ensure that his exclusive course would be one of the best in the world, the moneyman consulted more than half a dozen of the best golf course architects at the time. Talented designers like Charles B. Macdonald,

Donald Ross, A.W. Tillinghast, and H.S. Colt, to name just a few, were asked to lend their expertise to help him create a masterpiece. These gifted designers created a course that tempts those golfers wishing to test themselves. Pine Valley offers great challenges to even the best players. Each hole is different from the others, but somehow, they complement each other. Those who have played it note that there is not a bad hole.

Wondering why this exclusive club tucked away in the Garden State tops Augusta National and the Old Course at St. Andrews in the minds of many? Benjamin Smith, founder of "The Wandering Golfers" blog, offers this summation: "When it comes to the quality of the golf course, Pine Valley is rich in challenge, variety, and beauty: its cavernous bunkers are the stuff of legend, as is the fact this is generally viewed as one of the most difficult golf courses in the world.... This place is a bewitching blend of challenge and beauty, excitement and execution, mystique and peril."

Jack Nicklaus played the course on his honeymoon en route from New York City to Atlantic City. And, rumours are that nearly every U.S. president has played at least one round at Pine Valley, but it's impossible to say for sure whether or not this is true. The identity of the club's members (and guests) is a closely guarded secret. The Pine Valley police, formed in 1983 to protect the club and vet who comes in, guard entry from a small white house at the gate.

Hoping to get a tee time at this exclusive course? Good luck. It's not a place where money talks; instead, it's about who you know. Here's to hoping those connections you've worked so hard to make throughout your career are golfers who are somehow connected to — or know — a Pine Valley Golf Club member. Even connections aren't enough, though: only low-handicap players — a test needs to be taken to prove ability — are invited to become members. Oh, and another thing, only members are allowed to live in the town where the course is located.

Pine Valley is famously private, but for one day a year, the final Sunday in September, anyone is free to visit. No joke. The catch? You can't play the course, but you can walk it as you watch the final round of the Crump Cup, an amateur competition named after the man who designed the golf course.

It is a rare opportunity to pull back the curtain and walk these hallowed fairways. Spectators must park outside, along the road at the Splash Park. From there, a shuttle bus will take you through the gates. There are no ropes to hold the crowds back, but there are restrictions. You aren't allowed to take photographs, so cell phones and cameras are not permitted. But that's a gift; open your eyes and your ears, drink it all in — you'll never forget it.

I'LL HAVE A "SAND WEDGE," PLEASE

Modern golfers have Gene Sarazen, one of the top professional golfers of the 1920s and 1930s, to thank for inventing an essential piece of equipment found in most players' bags.

In 1935 Sarazen made what is considered one of the greatest shots in golf history — now immortalized as the "shot heard around the world" — when, using a 4-wood, he hit his second shot 225 yards to make a double-eagle on the par 5 fifteenth hole at the Masters. Three years before that, the game's first global superstar added another chapter to both his — and the game's — legacy when he won the British Open using what is believed to be the first sand wedge.

Sarazen started to tinker with the sole of what was then called a scoop club (to describe how the lofted club scooped a ball out of a bunker or deep rough). The idea of doing so came to the golfer one day while he received flying lessons from the American business magnate Howard Hughes. Sarazen observed how the airplane's tail adjusted during flight, lowering on take-off to help create lift for the aircraft. He wondered if this aerodynamic principle could be applied to a golf club to improve its lift. Sarazen figured he needed to lower the club more at the back of its sole to achieve the desired effect. So, he got a bundle of niblicks (equivalent to today's 9-iron) from Wilson Sporting Goods and began to reshape the clubs with a soldering iron — putting a flange on the back of the club to lower its centre of mass so this part of the club would hit the sand first. He also added extra lead to the front edge of the clubface, so it cut more smoothly through the sand.

Sarazen built his first prototype in 1931 and debuted this new club the following year at the British Open — he snuck the club past the tournament's officials because he thought they might deem what he started calling his "sand iron" illegal. That same year this club helped Sarazen win the U.S. Open.

Although he never patented his club, he was responsible for introducing the club he invented to the wider golf world. Sarazen had an endorsement contract with Wilson Sporting Goods — it lasted seventy-five years — and he persuaded the company to manufacture the sand wedge. The first clubs were introduced in 1933 as the Wilson R-90.

Sarazen's wedge revolutionized how we play golf today. It's fitting, therefore, that this first ever sand wedge resides today at the USGA Museum in Liberty Corner, New Jersey.

LORD BYRON AND A RIDICULOUS RECORD

It's a record that will probably never be broken. It is one of the most amazing feats not just in the annals of golf but also in the history of all professional sports.

Dominating the fairways and greens in an incomparable way, Texas golfer Byron Nelson began a winning streak on March 8, 1945, unlike any other seen before or since.

His incredible run of eleven victories in a row began in Miami at the International Four-Ball Championship and ended in August north of the border at the Canadian Open held at The Thornhill Club, where Nelson won by four. Before Nelson set this record, the record for most wins in a row by a PGA Tour player was three. In the seven plus decades since Byron accomplished his incredible feat, Tiger Woods is the only player who has come close to breaking that record. In 2006–7 he won seven consecutive tournaments during the PGA Tour season.

A few other fascinating facts to consider: of Nelson's 112 stroke-play rounds played in that record-setting season, ninety-two were below par. That achievement is even more incredible when you consider that he shot fifty below-par rounds in a row. As well as winning eleven tournaments in a row in the 1945 PGA Tour season, Nelson won an additional seven tournaments. In total, he won eighteen of the Tour's thirty scheduled events. Again, Woods is the only player in PGA Tour history to post comparable stats. In 2000 Tiger won nine of the twenty tournaments he entered, including three of the four majors.

Nelson's record is unlikely to ever be broken. There is remarkable parity among the golfers on the modern PGA Tour; this is illustrated by the fact that in the first eight events of the 2024 Tour season, three rookies won. No player today seems likely to seize golf's crown. Nelson's hold on it remains secure. Lord Byron: an apt nickname, indeed.

BREAKING BARRIERS

53

Shippen, Rhodes, Sifford, Elder, and Peete are players who deserve to be remembered. Before Tiger, they were the trailblazers that broke blatant colour barriers and racist segregation practices in golf.

In 1896 John Shippen (whose father was Black and whose mother was from Shinnecock Indian Nation — the official U.S. designation) made history when he played in the U.S. Open at Shinnecock Hills, where he worked as a caddie. He was able to play because club members had given him an exemption to compete. Not everyone was thrilled with this decision. Before the tournament started, many entrants sent the United States Golf Association (USGA) a petition objecting to "colored boys meeting them on equal terms." They threatened to withdraw, but the USGA held its ground and Shippen played; he even led after the first round. He ended up tying for sixth place and pocketed $10. Shippen went on to play in five more U.S. Opens.

After Shippen's success, it was more than a half-century before another Black golfer competed in the tournament. That honour goes to Ted Rhodes, who qualified for the 1948 U.S. Open, held at the Riviera Country Club in Los Angeles.

In 1928 Dewey Brown Sr. became the first Black PGA member. Just six years later, his PGA membership was revoked when the association implemented a "Caucasian-only" clause, which forbade anyone of African, Native American, Asian, or Latino background from joining the PGA of America. Brown did not let this racist prohibition keep him from the game he loved. He continued to play despite years of difficulties finding permanent employment in the golf industry because of this discrimination. In 1947 this trailblazer purchased the nine-hole Cedar River Golf Course, located in the Adirondacks, along with the small hotel on its property. A decade later, in 1958, Brown became the first Black member of the Golf Course Superintendents Association of America. Finally, in 1961, the PGA of America revoked the Caucasian-only clause and within five years, Brown was reinstated as a PGA professional.

Dr. Charles Sifford deserves special attention as a trail-blazer in professional golf. On March 28, 1960, Sifford, thirty-eight, became the first Black golfer to receive PGA Tour status. However, that achievement did not result in him being accorded all the rights given to others on the Tour. As a result of the entrenched racism that existed in the United States, where Jim Crow laws* were still in place in many Southern states, Sifford was not allowed to play in all Tour events until two years later. In 2004 Sifford became the first Black player enshrined in the World Golf Hall of Fame.

The first Black player to win a sanctioned PGA Tour event was Pete Brown, who won the 1964 Waco Turner Open. Although trailblazers like Brown were permitted to play in PGA Tour events, in the early years they faced considerable discrimination. They faced numerous restrictions — for example, since they were not allowed into the clubhouses of the private courses where these tournaments were played, they had to change their clothes in the parking lots.

Lee Elder played in the United Golfers Association (the equivalent to baseball's Negro Leagues, which existed from 1920 until the early 1950s) before joining the PGA Tour in 1968. He became the first Black person to play in the Masters in 1975 when he was forty years old! Even then, he faced racism. When his invitation arrived, Elder received death threats. However, he ignored them and played in the

---

* The Jim Crow laws that segregated Black people and denied them the same privileges in society as their white counterparts were not officially abolished until Lyndon B. Johnson enacted the Civil Rights Act in 1964.

tournament. He went on to play again; in total, he participated in the tournament six times.

Calvin Peete, born in Detroit, did not start playing golf until he was in his twenties, but he made the PGA Tour in 1975 and was the most successful Black golfer on the Tour until a guy named Tiger arrived. Peete won twelve tournaments, took the Vardon Trophy in 1984 for the lowest scoring average, and also led the PGA Tour in driving accuracy for ten straight years.

In 2019 Elder was interviewed by *Golf Digest* about his experience competing in that first Masters. Reflecting on it, he said, "The display from the employees of Augusta National was especially moving. Most of the staff was Black, and on Friday, they left their duties to line the 18th fairway as I walked toward the green. I couldn't hold back the tears. Of all the acknowledgments of what I had accomplished by getting there, this one meant the most."

In 2021 Elder returned to Augusta to act as an honorary starter. He joined Jack Nicklaus and Gary Player, hitting the ceremonial tee shot before the official tournament began.

Not only were Black players excluded from the Tour, they were regularly excluded from clubs across the United States. It was only in 1990 that Ron Townsend was admitted as the first Black member of Augusta National — no official clause barred Black people from competing, either, but unofficially they were not allowed. Before Elder, the only Black people at the Masters were the caddies employed by the club.

As a result of their exclusion from the established clubs, Black people created their own. The first Black-owned golf club in the United States, opened in 1920, was the Shady Rest Golf and Country Club, located in Scotch Plains, New Jersey.

PERSONAL PLAYGROUNDS OF THE UBER RICH

Tired of waking up early and logging on to your computer to try to secure a tee time two weeks away at your favourite course? Slow play or some other minor grievance at your club so bad that it is driving you mad to the point you are ready to quit not just the club but the game? Thinking things might be better if you joined an exclusive club — if you had the money to do that? There are exclusive golf clubs ... and then there are exclusive golf courses — private playgrounds where the owner is the only member.

One of the first of these courses was built by T. Suffern Tailer, a New York banker. He was a member of Newport Country Club but became disappointed with the quality of the course and following the introduction of the first rubber-wound golf balls, which flew so much farther than the balls previously used, he found its short length no longer challenging. When his club had no interest in making the changes he suggested, Tailer purchased seventy acres next to the Newport club. The land was spread out over four separate lots that did not adjoin. Needless to say, fashioning a course on the land made for a unique design challenge. So, Tailer hired acclaimed architect Charles B. Macdonald to create his private playground. The nine-hole course, named Ocean Links, opened in July 1921. Tailer paid for the upkeep of the course out of his own pocket and generously allowed his former pals at Newport Country Club next door to play his private course whenever they wanted. After Tailer passed away in 1928, despite setting up a trust fund to keep the course going, his family sold the course in 1931.

On the California coast, a Hollywood silent film star created another private club. Harold Lloyd was a huge star in his day, rivalling Charlie Chaplin in popularity. He was also an astute businessman. He owned all the films he starred in and so received 80 percent of the profits they made. It's estimated that by 1929 he had made the equivalent of $2.1 billion in today's dollars. When he built his lavish estate, which he called Greenacres, he, like Tailer, built his own personal golf course. The official name of this short course built for one was the Harold Lloyd Golf Course, but the movie mogul called it "Safety Last!" named after one of his hit movies. After his death in 1971, the house, including the grounds and the course, was opened to tourists. A few years later, however, it was auctioned off, and Safety Last! was no more.

Retired National Basketball Association legend Michael Jordan owns another one of these courses. Playing on it, he has a lifetime guarantee that he can have whatever tee time he wants. Called Grove XXIII (a reference to the number he wore on his jerseys for most of his career), the course, situated on two-hundred-plus acres of a former citrus grove, is found on the outskirts of Hobe Sound, Florida. Bobby Weed was hired to build this dream eighteen, which also includes a practice facility that would be the envy of most private clubs — two four-hundred-yard, double-sided driving ranges with target greens, along with a putting green that is split into four quadrants, each with a different slope. The course officially opened in 2019.

GOLF OBSESSED IN THE LAND OF ICE

Surprisingly, Iceland boasts more golf courses per capita than any other country in the world. Located just below the Arctic Circle, the small island nation, which has a population of only 388,000 people, is home to sixty-five golf courses. That's one course for every six thousand Icelanders. Yes, the season is short — late May to early September — but when Iceland's courses are open, you can literally play all day and all night. Ever wanted to tee off at midnight? In Iceland, you can. Between early June and late July, the country enjoys almost perpetual daylight, thanks to its northerly location, and so its courses are able to remain open twenty-four hours a day.

Reykjavik Golf Club, Iceland's oldest club, opened in 1934 in the capital city. Outside of the capital, many of the nation's courses offer breathtaking views, with dormant volcanoes on one side and the Atlantic Ocean on the other.

The country is also home to one of the world's northernmost golf courses: Akureyri Golf Club. Since 1986, this high-altitude club, a four hours' drive north of the capital, has hosted the Arctic Open. A popular thirty-six-hole tournament, it attracts golfers from around the globe to compete in this unique event where tee times occur after midnight.

Some golf-mad Icelanders not satisfied with playing only in the short summer season are known to play snow golf up in the mountains of these islands using colourful balls and designing their own holes.

THE WANDERLUST GOLFER

Over fifty-five thousand kilometres travelled, forty-
one states and 580 different courses visited, and 10,440
holes played. That's one epic golf journey.

For the love of the game or just ridiculous? In 2023
American golf photographer and blogger Patrick Koenig
set a new Guinness World Record for the most eighteen
hole golf courses played in one year. On a journey that he
dubbed the RGV Tour, he travelled from course to course
in a fully outfitted and customized "recreational golf
vehicle" (RGV). Along the way, he hosted a podcast from
the RGV and raised $40,000 for the First Tee of Greater
Seattle, a youth development organization that provides
children with life-enhancing experiences through golf,
and a few other local charities.

Overcoming the elements, mental fatigue, and a couple of RGV breakdowns, the forty-four-year-old Californian smashed the previous record of 449 courses visited set by Canadian couple Jonathan and Cathie Weaver in 2009. Koenig broke this record with seventy-eight days to spare, surpassing the Weavers' record in October at the Interlocken Golf Club in Colorado.

Koenig relied on passion, planning, and perseverance to complete this golf odyssey. Averaging 1.6 rounds per day, he sometimes played thirty-six or fifty-four holes in one twenty-four-hour stretch — and often more than one course in a day — to keep his record-setting pace. The place where he played the most holes in one day, which he compared to running a marathon, was Miami, Florida, where he played all seventy-two holes at Trump National Doral Golf Club.

Koenig walked for 2,450 of the kilometres he travelled, or 70 percent of his rounds — a distance roughly equal to fifty-eight marathons or the distance between Los Angeles and Houston.

Reflecting on this record-setting year-long golf adventure, Koenig called it a "ridiculous ride." And in an interview with CNN, he claimed that "total enlightenment maybe still eludes me, but this was a good step towards finding that."

A TRIPLE BOGEY YOU WANT

Geoff Tait was sitting on his front porch in Toronto's Beaches neighborhood in early 2013, doing some late afternoon soul searching. His multi-million-dollar golf apparel business (Quagmire, maker of Arnie Wear) had started to fall apart the year before. When the business dissolved, the entrepreneur was left to figure out what was next.

Although he had a couple of good job offers — both in and outside the golf industry — on the table, Tait knew he still wanted to be his own boss. His love of beer and a desire to stay in the industry he enjoyed led to the creation of Triple Bogey. In 2013 Tait manufactured some proto-type cans and brewed the first small batch of this craft beer. With its launch the following year, Triple Bogey became the first brewery in Canada to market beer directly to the golf industry.

A marketing guru, Tait knew that for his product to be successful and penetrate new markets, he needed a fun name for it — something everyone could connect with. He picked Triple Bogey as the moniker because he understood the brand name would market itself. As he says, "It's something nobody is trying to get, but they all want to drink one!" His approach springs from his philosophy about life: "It's too short and it's too serious."

Thanks to the golf industry network he developed during his Quagmire days, he managed to pick up a few accounts right away. This gave Tait confidence to buy a couple of delivery trucks and hire a driver. In the first few years, he and his wife ran the business, with Geoff taking orders and printing up invoices in the morning and then hitting the road and delivering beer to licensees in the afternoon. His wife helped with the bookkeeping and worked at various promotional events. Drawing on his experience with Quagmire, Geoff eventually expanded Triple Bogey's offerings and added a fun and edgy apparel line. The slogan? Fit for the fairways.

A decade after Geoff and Megan launched their Canadian craft beer, Triple Bogey has grown. Eight other employees now work with the couple. In 2023 sales surpassed 5.6 million cans. Along with the original premium lager, the company offers several other beers (including a non-alcoholic option) and a variety of ready-to-drink vodka cocktails called Transfusions. Triple Bogey's products are now served at over four hundred golf courses and more than eight hundred locations.

A PANDEMIC BUMP

March 11, 2020, is a day no one will ever forget. On this late winter day, the World Health Organization declared Covid-19 a global pandemic. With this announcement, the offices of governments and businesses around the world shut down. Overnight, people were sent home from their jobs. They were told to stay "locked down" in quarantine to help prevent the virus from spreading further. Fear was the initial response. It was followed by feelings of being lost and lonely as the imposed isolation order dragged on from days to weeks to months.

Businesses suffered, especially those in the food, beverage, hospitality, and tourism industries, since they all rely on people being there for their survival. When things finally started to open up, golf, which prior to the pandemic had been declining in popularity, was one of the activities deemed safe to participate in at a "social distance." New, temporary rules were implemented, and temporary changes were made to courses: ball washers, the rakes in the bunkers, and even the flagsticks in the holes were removed. Celebratory actions such as high-fives were prohibited. All of this was done to make sure the virus didn't spread.

So, while many industries struggled and small businesses — even with government aid and loans — closed, unable to survive the toll of this pandemic, golf saw an explosion in business. During those times of fear and uncertainty, many found a brief respite from the sense of isolation and claustrophobia they were feeling in playing a round. Golf proved the perfect pastime; it enabled people to see friends and socialize at a time when many other activities were cancelled or temporarily on hold.

The private club I worked at saw its tee sheet booked solid from 7:00 a.m. to 7:00 p.m. This trend played out in Canada from St. John's to Victoria; the story was the same all across the United States. Some golf clubs saw as much as a 25 percent increase in rounds played. Many of these players were newcomers to the sport. According to the U.S.-based National Golf Foundation, more than three million new golfers tried the game for the first time during the pandemic. The only time North America saw more new golfers was following Tiger Woods's historic win at the 1997 Masters. The pandemic caused a bump in the popularity of golf as people sought a pastime that they could take part in safely, and with that came a similar spike in equipment sales.

59

SILENT SANDY

While he became known as "Silent Sandy" — a nickname bestowed upon him at the 1933 British Amateur for his quiet demeanour — when Charles Ross Somerville stepped on a golf course, he let his clubs speak for him.

Born May 4, 1903, in London, Ontario, the Canadian is known for a couple of firsts. Somerville was a natural athlete. Before choosing golf as his main sport, he turned down offers from both of Toronto's professional teams: the Argonauts (football) and the Maple Leafs (hockey). Once he committed to the game, Somerville dominated the amateur golf circuit in Canada throughout the 1920s and 1930s. He won six Canadian Amateur titles and was runner-up four times. He also won the Ontario Amateur four times. What really cemented his place in the annals of golf — and why the

Canadian Press named him the Golfer of the Half-Century in 1950 — is the feat he accomplished in Baltimore in 1932.

On a mid-September day, at the Five Farms Course, Somerville, twenty-nine years old, defeated American Johnny Goodman of Omaha, Nebraska, two and one* in the match play final of the U.S. Amateur to become the first international player to win the Havemeyer Trophy — the most prized title in all of amateur golf. A shocked and humble Somerville received a three-minute standing ovation from the throngs around the final green.

The second record Somerville holds is not as well known. He achieved it two years later in Georgia. Bobby Jones, the great American amateur golfer and co-founder of the Masters, invited his good friend to the inaugural Masters tournament in 1934 when it was called the Augusta National Invitational.

On the 145-yard, par 3 sixteenth hole, using a hickory-shafted club with an iron clubface (known as a "mashie niblick" and equivalent to the modern 7-iron), Somerville recorded the first-ever hole-in-one in Masters history.

Silent off the course, Somerville's on-course feats were heard around the world. The gentleman golfer passed away May 17, 1991, but the mark he left on the game is forever remembered.

---

* The score "two and one" means that the winner is two holes ahead with one hole to play (the match ends after the seventeenth hole).

THE AMATEUR QUEEN

The first — and only — Canadian golfer inducted into the World Golf Hall of Fame is Marlene Stewart Streit, who was added in 2004. There are very few women's amateur golf competitions she has not won in her storied career. Many of these she won multiple times, including eleven Canadian Opens. She is also the only Canadian woman to capture the Canadian, British, Australian, and U.S. Amateur titles.

Ageless. At eighty years old, the Canadian legend still played and regularly shot her age. A decade before, just six months shy of her seventieth, Streit won the 2003 U.S. Senior Women's Amateur Championship (a competition open to women fifty and older). Streit defeated opponents in the semi-final and final who were a combined twenty-seven years her junior. With this feat, Streit added yet another record: she became the oldest player ever to win a United States Golf Association championship.

Streit won her first big event and came to national prominence in 1951 when, as a seventeen-year-old, she won both the Canadian Open and "Closed" (an event for Canadians only) trophies. In 2000 Streit was named the Canadian Ladies' Golf Association player of the twentieth century. She is a member of both the Canadian Golf Hall of Fame and the World Golf Hall of Fame.

Wonder why she never turned professional? Mainly a fear of flying — after surviving a plane crash, she became a reluctant flyer. This, of course, limited her ability to compete. How would she have done as a professional? JoAnne Gunderson Carner, who Streit beat for her first U.S. Amateur title in 1956 and who went on to win forty-three titles on the Ladies Professional Golf Organization Tour, once said that if her good friend had turned pro, "She would've needed a truck to take her money to the bank."

Dedication and determination combined with unbridled passion for the game. That's what defined Marlene Stewart Streit; it's no wonder she has remained an inspiration to generation after generation of players.

THE GODFATHER OF GOLF WRITING

Golf is a sport that has inspired many writers. There are probably thousands of works of non-fiction about the sport — books on the game itself, histories of courses, biographies of famous players, instructional guides. Many novels also feature the game. There are even poems that have been written about golf. Since the Scots invented the game hundreds of years ago, golf has fascinated writers. In researching and writing this book, I relied on my personal golf library, which numbers in the hundreds, to dig out many of the fascinating facts found in these pages. There are certain books and certain writers that stand out — in particular, the triumvirate of Bernard Darwin, Henry Longhurst, and Herbert Warren Wind.

Darwin was one of the first true golf writers. His grandfather was the famous scientist Charles Darwin, but Bernard was more interested in playing sports than studying nature. Not only was he a great writer, Darwin was also a fine player — he captained the golf team during his university years at Cambridge. During his brief career as a lawyer — he detested the law — he was offered the opportunity to sub in as a journalist for a friend one day. After covering one match, he was hooked. Writing about the game became his vocation. He was so good that the *Times* hired him as their golf correspondent. Darwin created a new style of reporting. His descriptions of matches were cinematic in scope, colourful, and literary. He laced his pieces with quotes from writers he admired like Charles Dickens. His work was groundbreaking.

Herbert Warren Wind is known today as the father of American golf writers. Well educated, Wind graduated from Yale and had a master's degree from Cambridge. His love of chronicling the game began in 1941 when he first starting writing about the sport for the *New Yorker*, where he was a staff writer for seven years. Wind later wrote for *Sports Illustrated* and *Golf Digest*, and he published or edited more than a dozen books over the course of a fifty-year golf writing career — covering all aspects of the game. As professional Ben Crenshaw said, following the writer's passing, "Every time you read him, you get a history lesson, a golf lesson and a life lesson."

In 1992 the PGA presented Wind with its lifetime achievement award, and the United States Golf Association names its annual book award after the writer. Following his death in 2005, Wind was inducted into the World Golf Hall of Fame.

England's Henry Longhurst matched Wind's longevity — and dedication to writing powerful prose about the grand old game. He was the *Sunday Times'* golf reporter for forty-five years and was also a regular contributor to *Golf Illustrated*. In 2017 he was inducted into the World Golf Hall of Fame. Longhurst was a regular covering the Masters as the senior commentator for the BBC. His memoir, *My Life and Soft Times*, gives a taste of his prose. In it, you'll find some of his most famous quotes about the game, such as "playing golf is such as learning a foreign language."

62 BESPOKE BEAUTIES

Ready to make a golden statement and bring some bling to your game? The Japanese have you covered.

For that golden touch from tee to green, look no further than Honma Golf, specifically its BERES luxury line of premium hand-crafted clubs. BERES clubs feature bedazzling design. The BERES line is built exclusively by *takumi*, Japanese artisans who have at least twenty to thirty years' experience. Producing these clubs is an art these craftsmen take seriously. Clubs are designed to exact specifications: special steel is used; five or six coats of paint 0.07 millimetres thick are applied to each club; and they are polished in increments of 0.01 millimetres. It's no wonder that these clubs are the clubs of choice of many Hollywood stars and heads of state.

What is the cost of the highest tier of Honma's BERES line? Expect to shell out up to $70,000 for a set of these bespoke beauties. Given the price, I don't think I would risk hitting a ball with these clubs — I would be too afraid of scratching them. Playing with such luxurious golf clubs would feel like using your fine china for your toddler's birthday party. Then again, these Honma clubs are several tax brackets out of my price range, so what do I know?

The exclusive sixtieth anniversary set, released in 2017, has gold and platinum plating. But these luxurious clubs are not just pretty — Honma clubs are also incredibly durable. They are so strong, in fact, that they can survive the mighty jaws of an alligator. A story posted to the company's U.S. website tells about how after a Florida man's Honma driver flew out of his hands into a pond where a hungry alligator chomped on it and then spit it out, it was retrieved with nothing but a few scratches on it.

Other luxury Japanese golf brands include XXIO, Miura, and Ryoma.

Eccentric Texan billionaire and visionary entrepreneur Bob Parsons founded PXG — the only non-Japanese high-end golf manufacturer — in 2013. In a recent interview, Parsons boasted that PXG makes the very best equipment in the industry and shared how their line of Gen6 irons are forged five times and they're milled — something no other manufacturer does. Although this luxury brand is not Japanese, in 2024 Parsons's company announced the opening of its first flagship location, PXG Aoyama, in the greater Tokyo area.

TREVINO AND A $55 PUTTER

No piece of equipment in a golfer's bag is as personal as the putter. Players kiss this flat stick when their
putts are pure and roll regularly into the hole; they throw
it, curse it, and trash it for another when the balls miss the
cup more often than they drop in.

Modern putters come in all kinds of different shapes
and sizes, and every year brings new designs that promise
to help golfers sink more putts. Ping is the industry leader,
and its Anser model has more worldwide victories attached
to it than any other putter. However, there are many other
makes and models that have their devotees. For most golfers, the choice of putter has nothing to do with the cost or
make of the club. It's all about feel. Some like their putters short; some like them long — that's me. (Using a short

putter, I got the dreaded yips. The moment I switched to a long putter my stroke improved and so did my enjoyment of the game.) Some people use the same putter for most of their careers; others change them as frequently as people replace their toothbrush.

Here's a fun story about Lee Trevino and a putter. His wife bought him a $55 Ping A-Blade putter in the club's pro shop after a woeful day of putting — taking thirty-six strokes in the first round — at the Dutch Open in 1984. The next day, after doing a little customization by stomping on it on the concrete a few times, he used this gift from his wife. Trevino putted the lights out, shooting 64 to win the tournament. In the mid-1980s, Trevino was not entering as many tournaments. He was found more often in the broadcast booth, working as a TV commentator, than on the golf course competing in a PGA Tour event. But this putter gave him the desire to play more. In eleven rounds following that win in the Netherlands, Trevino was fifty-two under par. His new-found success on the green allowed him to score a fourth-place finish in the Buick Open.

Since he had an exemption as a past winner, he decided to play in the 1984 PGA Championship at Shoal Creek Club in Alabama. He believed his confident putting stroke could help him make the leader board. And, you guessed it, that Ping putter propelled the forty-four-year-old to win his sixth major championship and his final win on the PGA Tour.

64

THE STYMIE

Golf has gifted many words to the English lan-
guage; "stymie" is perhaps one of the most useful. The
word entered the English language as a noun, used for the
situation when a player's ball lies between another player's
ball and the hole — the player can't sink their putt without smashing into their opponent's ball. The word began to
be used as a transitive verb: to "stymie" someone meant to
block or impede their action. The verb could be used in any
situation — on or off the course.

Most often, these stymies happened by accident, but
golfers sometimes tried to deliberately stymie their opponent on a long putt to give themselves an advantage on the
green. These stymies led to some golfers trying shots like
those used in billiards, since in the early days of the game

the rules stated that the golfer who was stymied had to try and chip, slice, or hook their putt around the ball blocking their path to the hole.

The term is now obsolete, at least in golf. In 1952 the two governing bodies of the game (the United States Golf Association and the R&A) revised the rules to eliminate the possibility of a stymie occurring. Golfers today mark their ball if it is in the way of their playing partner, so the problem no longer exists.

TO RUSSIA WITH GOLF DREAMS

Despite boasting the largest land area of any coun-try in the world, Russia has very few golf courses. The sport is not as popular there as it is in the rest of Europe or any of the other two-hundred-plus countries in the world where it is enjoyed. There are a few reasons. First, the perception that golf is bourgeois. Golf's popularity in the West impeded the development of the sport in the country for most of the twentieth century. Although a few courses were built in the nineteenth century, they disappeared following the Russian Revolution. The Bolsheviks weren't interested in the game. It was only following the demise of the Soviet Union in the 1990s that golf was reintroduced to the country. Second, the weather. Russian winters are long; summers are short. The golf seasons are necessarily brief. Lastly, cost. Although there are a number of oligarchs in Russia, there isn't a big middle class. So, the number of people who can afford to play is limited.

The first modern golf course built in Russia was the nine-hole Moscow City Golf Club, which opened in 1989. Its creation was only possible because of *glasnost* (the opening up of the U.S.S.R. to outsiders under the rule of President Mikhail Gorbachev). Swedish hockey player Sven Johannsson convinced the government to let him build the course, and in doing so, he re-established golf in Russia. The Moscow City GC was followed by the country's first championship eighteen-hole private course — Moscow Country Club. Built on the outskirts of the city, it opened in 1993.

From these beginnings, the number of courses in Russia has expanded to more than thirty. Still small for such a large country. Data from the Russian Golf Association, dated from 2020, stated there were 130,000 people playing golf. However, this number included the 100,000 kids who receive some form of coaching on the sport in Russian schools. While the overall number of golfers may still be small, the fact that there are so many people learning the game bodes well for its future. As well, American firms like Jack Nicklaus Design and English architects like Nick Faldo have been hired in recent years to build courses in Russia, proof that while it is still in its infancy, golf is a growing sport.

THE OLD AND THE YOUNG

In the history of golf, there is no father and son pair like Old Tom Morris and Young Tom Morris. Each left a lasting legacy on the game.

Thomas Mitchell Morris, better known as Old Tom Morris, was born in 1821 in St. Andrews. He fell in love with golf from a young age — he started playing at age ten with wine-bottle corks pierced with nails to serve as balls. He started an apprenticeship with a local club maker. Old Tom also caddied and was a decent golfer — he won the Scottish Open four times.

Old Tom was the first Keeper of the Green, a job he performed at both Prestwick Golf Club in Ayrshire and at the Old Course at St. Andrews. He began his career at the Royal and Ancient Golf Club in 1864 and remained in that position for thirty-nine years. He is responsible for many of the fundamental agronomic practices today's superintendents use to maintain their golf courses. Top-dressing greens with sand to aid the growth of the turf was Morris's innovation. He was also the first to use a push mower to cut greens.

At the Old Course, Old Tom worked as both the greenskeeper and a golf club maker; he even designed several golf courses. When he retired in 1904, the R&A paid him a good pension. In his later years, he became a bit of a celebrity, well known in the tourist town of St. Andrews.

His eldest son, Young Tom Morris, was born in 1851 and he eventually went into the "family business." He was an even better player than his old man and won his first British Open in 1868 at age seventeen. Young Tom proceeded to repeat this feat for the next three years. Sadly, he did not live that much longer. Young Tom died, unofficially from a broken heart after losing his wife earlier in the year, at only twenty-four years old, on Christmas Day, 1875.

THE NICKNAME GAME

From the Bambino in baseball to the Great One in hockey to Dr. J in basketball, nicknames for the greats in these games are intertwined with the history of their respective sports. Golf is no different. A colourful collection of monikers, like the Shark and the Walrus, have been coined for some of its most famous players. Here are a few of the most famous and fun.

Tiger: Few people even know his real name. Born Eldrick Woods, he was given this nickname by his father, who gave it to his son in memory of a Vietnamese soldier friend.

The Golden Bear: Jack Nicklaus's nickname referred to his blond hair, the aggressive way he played, and also to his golden touch (he won piles of money in his professional career).

Aquaman: American Woody Austin was given this moniker after he fell into a pond next to the fourteenth green at Royal Montreal during the 2007 Presidents Cup. In his singles match against Argentine Angel Cabrera the following day, Austin hammed it up for the fans, wearing a pair of scuba googles as he walked off the fourteenth tee. The new name stuck.

Mrs. 59: The only player to ever shoot 59 on the Ladies Professional Golf Organization (LPGA) Tour, Swedish golfer Annika Sorenstam was given the nickname "Mrs. 59."

The Big Easy: The former world number one, South African golfer Ernie Els got this name because he is tall, and his swing looks so effortless.

Pink Panther: The American LPGA player Paula Creamer got this moniker when she was sixteen simply because of her love of the color pink.

Big Mama: JoAnne Carner, who won an astounding forty-three LPGA events, including a pair of U.S. Opens, got this nickname due to her tall and powerful frame.

Fuzzy: Frank Urban Zoeller, who won a pair of majors (the U.S. Open and the Masters), got this handle simply because of his initials: F.U.Z.

The Great White Shark: One of my favourite players when I was a kid, Australian Greg Norman, got this name after an exchange with a reporter at the 1981 Masters. In the interview, he described his upbringing diving among sharks on the Great Barrier Reef. This fact when combined with his flowing blond hair and an aggressive go-for-broke playing style made the connection an obvious one. The appearance of the headline "Great White Shark Leads U.S. Masters" in the *Atlanta Constitution* confirmed the nickname.

The Walrus: This is one of the not-so-nice nicknames. Craig Stadler was given it for his physical appearance; slightly overweight, he sported a moustache that resembled the whiskers of this marine mammal. That look and his fiery temper earned him a name that didn't suggest much admiration.

FLUBS, CHUNKS, AND SHANKS

Golf is known to cause many a player to curse when they hit a bad shot. Yes, it's a frustrating game. And yes, it is really hard. So, it's no wonder that a colourful collection of terms has been created to describe unwanted shots. Here are just a few:

> banana ball (a curving slice)
> blade (a shot where the club hits the top half of the ball)
> block (an inside-out swing path that causes a slice)
> chunk (a mis-hit where the club hits the ground before the ball)
> chilli-dip (a chunk shot with a wedge)

dub (a chunk where the club hits the top
    half of the ball)
duck hook (an extreme version of a hook)
duff (another name for a chunk)
E.A. (elephant's ass — a shot that flies high
    but doesn't travel far)
fat (a chunk in which a lot of grass and dirt
    comes between the club and the ball)
flub (the general term for a bad shot)
fluff (moving a ball to get a better lie)
shank (hitting the ball off the heel of the
    club instead of the clubface; also called
    a hosel rocket or skank)
skull (a shot where the edge of the club hits
    the middle of the ball)
whiff (a shot in which the golfer misses the
    ball completely)
yips (a shot affected by involuntary wrist
    spasms)

While hackers are more likely to hit one of these dreaded shots, professionals hit these unwanted shots also. During the 2023 Solheim Cup, a biennial transatlantic match-play event between the best twelve players from the Ladies European Tour and the best twelve from the Ladies Professional Golf Organization, Lexi Thompson hit a shank that left even the announcers speechless. The twenty-eight-year-old's shot went straight right and hit her playing partner and caddie! *Golfweek* writer Beth Ann Nichols captured this incident with the following tweet: "Golf, man. One minute you're driving the green from over 300 yards and the next you're shanking a chip and feeling like you're standing there naked in front of the world."

Another of these dreaded shots that definitely make you feel small is the chunk — when you hit too far behind the ball causing it to land well short of your intended target. One of the most famous chunks occurred at the 2016 Masters. In the final round, Jordan Spieth was leading on the back 9 and looked like a lock to win a second straight Green Jacket until disaster struck on the par 3 twelfth hole. Spieth chunked two balls in a row into the water and eventually made a quadruple bogey.

Finally, something I'm unfortunately most familiar with: the yips. These are involuntary wrist spasms that happen most often when putting, but they can also occur when chipping. This neurological condition affects athletes in other sports. Researchers at the Mayo Clinic found that 33 percent to 48 percent of all serious golfers have experienced the yips at some point. Hank Haney, who once coached Tiger Woods, battled the yips for twenty years before finding a solution.

THE THREE-FINGERED MAN OF STEEL

Billy Burke had six top tens in major champion-
ships. His lone win came at the 1931 U.S. Open. Today, this
tournament is sometimes dubbed the "Inferno at Inverness"
because it was played in Inverness, Ohio, in an early July
heatwave that saw temperatures approach 38°C (exceeding
100°F).

The dramatic finale of this major generated its own kind
of heat. After four rounds and seventy-two holes, Burke was
tied with George Von Helm — the PGA Tour's leading
money winner heading into the tournament. Von Helm
sank a ten-foot putt on the last hole to tie Burke. The United
States Golf Association (USGA), which ran the tournament, decided that a thirty-six-hole playoff would decide
the winner. The only problem was that the pair were still

tied when — you guessed it — Von Helm made another ten-footer on the last hole. So, for the third day in a row, these tired golfers battled for another thirty-six holes, trading the lead twenty-five times. Finally, Burke triumphed, coming out the victor by a single stroke.

His win was remarkable considering he had only three fingers on his left hand — he lost the other two in a workplace accident when he was a teenager working at the same iron foundry where his dad was employed. The loss forced him to adapt his golf grip.

But the most historic and fascinating fact about Burke's only major championship win is that he became the first golfer to win the U.S. Open using steel-shafted clubs. A.G. Spalding and Brothers had introduced a signature set of Bobby Jones irons, with steel shafts painted brown to make them look more like hickory, in late 1930, and Burke proved their proficiency when he captured the 1931 U.S. Open with a set of these new-fangled clubs. Burke's victory played a pivotal role in the wider adoption of steel-shafted clubs, which eventually overtook hickory sticks. Popular because of their endurance, reliability, and relatively low cost, the new clubs were particularly liked because they helped golfers hit farther.

While the steel shaft didn't catch on until the 1930s, it was patented as far back as 1910, created by a General Electric engineer named Arthur F. Knight. It took quite some time not only to fine-tune a way to manufacture and mass produce these new clubs. It also took time to convince golf's governing bodies that they were good for the game.

The USGA banned steel shafts in 1923, declaring that they might be a "mechanical aid." After further study, they approved them for tournament play the following year. In 1929, after the R&A approved steel shafts, golfers around the world began replacing their hickory-shafted clubs with more durable and distance-yielding steel ones.

Steel-shafted clubs became the standard until the graphite-shafted ones (first invented by Frank Thomas for Shakespeare Sporting Goods in 1969 — a company better known for its fishing equipment) replaced them. This change did not happen quickly, though; they were not adopted by golf manufacturers until the 1990s, when changes in technology allowed them to produce them at a (relatively) low cost. Rich Beem was the first professional player to claim a major championship using graphite-shafted irons when he won the 2022 PGA Championship.

70

A NEED FOR SPEED

I dread getting caught behind slow golfers. As a teenager, my friend and I joked about the "turtle family" we sometimes got stuck behind. And, playing solo, to fit in a few more holes before darkness descends, I've jogged from shot to shot with my carry bag bouncing on my back. No Zen golf for me, but even my fastest rounds have nothing on golfers that possess a need for speed.

The game is, by its nature, relatively leisurely — the average time to complete eighteen holes is four and a half hours. So, imagine finishing that same round in the amount of time it takes most golfers to complete just two holes. According to the *Guinness Book of World Records*, the fastest round of golf by an individual is twenty-seven minutes and nine seconds. James Carvill achieved this at Warrenpoint Golf Course in Northern Ireland in 1987.

The nine-hole speed record belongs to speed golfer Luke Willett. In November 2023, running and sweating between swings, the Brit — known as "the Iron Golfer" for his many extraordinary fairway feats — played nine holes in twenty minutes and twelve seconds using only a 3-wood, a 6-iron, and a pitching wedge.

In the world of professional golf, Sweden's Sebastian Söderberg, playing solo in the final round of the Dubai Desert Classic in 2020, holds the record. He completed eighteen holes in one hour and thirty-five minutes — the fastest round recorded in a European Tour competition. In North America, the record on the PGA Tour is held by Wesley Bryan, who, during the final round of the 2017 BMW Championship at Conway Farms, basically ran a 13.5-minute mile. Bryan played eighteen holes in eighty-nine minutes and still shot a two-under 69 that included fourteen pars, one birdie, and one bogey. The PGA Tour pro averaged about a stroke a minute and approximately five minutes per hole.

This professional record most likely will never be broken, since it's rare for PGA Tour players to go out as a single. In 2021, at the Tour Championship at East Lake Golf Club in Atlanta, Georgia, Chilean Joaquin Niemann tried to match Bryan's feat. First, some context. The Tour Championship is the final event of the PGA Tour's season-long points race to win the FedEx Cup. There is up to

$75 million in bonus money available to win. This final event features only thirty players. Entering the final round, Niemann was twenty-four shots off the lead and knew the chances of him making up much ground were slim. So, teeing off as a single, he decided instead to have some fun and pick up the pace. His caddie, Gary Matthews, emptied his golf bag to get it to a more manageable twelve kilos, light enough to allow him to hoof it and keep up with his boss. About thirty to forty college kids ran with him for the last five holes — a stretch Niemann called a "blur." PGA Tour officials had some fun of their own at Niemann's expense, pulling a prank he initially fell for. The Tour representative told him he had disrespected the game and that he would, as a result, face a $10,000 fine. Of course, he was never asked to pay it.

For players with a real need for speed — not just occasionally, but for every round — there is a league. Speed golf was created by American Steve Scott in 1979 when the former mile record holder sped around a California course in twenty-nine minutes and thirty-three seconds playing with only a 3-iron. Today, there are speed golf leagues throughout North America, Europe, and Japan. The sport's inaugural world championships were held in 2012 at Bandon Dunes Golf Resort in Bandon, Oregon. One key to succeeding in speed golf is to travel light; most players carry between four and seven clubs. Scores in this variation of golf are determined by combining the number of strokes taken with the amount of time it takes to complete one's round.

71
COLD CLUBBING

In most of North America, golfers empty their bags and hibernate in the winter— maybe playing some virtual golf at a local simulator. Some vacation in southern climes so that they can get a few rounds in. There are others, though, that are so dedicated to the sport that they will not let winter get in the way of them enjoying a game. For them, snowfalls and swings go together. Who is crazy enough to play when temperatures drop below zero? Fanatics who enjoy a round of snow golf. Me, I'm a fair-weather golfer. Usually, my limit is 10°C (50°F), but there are others who are so golf-obsessed they'll throw on an extra layer or two of clothing and hit the tee.

Snow golf requires special equipment, like rubber tees that sit on top of the frozen ground. And obviously, it's not possible to follow all of the official rules of the game. For example, there are no penalties for losing your ball, and once on the green, two putts are the maximum you can take.

Since players are usually putting on an icy green, closest to the pin usually rules the day. Sinking the ball into the cup doesn't happen often. Although it began as a niche activity, snow golf is becoming more popular. Many resort and daily-fee courses in North America are now remaining open during the winter months to accommodate this trend.

A couple of advantages of golfing in the winter: green fees are usually reduced, and there is no difficulty getting a tee time. So, next winter, grab your toque, layer — and limber — up, and hit your local course for some frozen fun.

GOING FOR THE GREEN ... LAND

You would think that an island with the word green in its name would definitely be an ideal home to golf. That is until you learn that Greenland — the world's largest island (it is three times the size of Texas) — has an ice sheet covering more than four-fifths of its total land area. Sparsely populated, mostly due to its climate and isolation, two-thirds of the island lies within the Article Circle and at its northernmost point, it is less than eight hundred kilometres from the North Pole.

However, as snow golf enthusiasts will attest, you do not always need green greens to enjoy a game of golf. In Greenland, these putting surfaces are known as "whites." What you do need, especially in the northernmost part of the island, is a lot of layers of clothing to keep warm and a brightly coloured pink or orange ball so you do not lose it in the sea of white that makes up some of the makeshift courses. One unique rule to know: you get a free drop if you hit within ten metres of an iceberg! And yes, there is a chance a polar bear might eat your ball. Frostbite is also another possible hazard of a game of golf in Greenland.

Since 1997, the island has hosted the annual World Ice Golf Championship in the northwest town of Uummannaq, which holds the Guinness Record for the world's northernmost golf course.

73
PUTT, PUTT, PUTT

Earlier in this book, you read the story of a golfer who plays — not just plays but wins tournaments — with only a putter. But for the rest of those who golf, that piece of equipment is reserved for the green. And there is nothing as satisfying as wielding that stick to sink a long putt. In my day, I've made a few from more than fifty feet, but that's nothing compared to the following record.

Jay Stocki, a semi-retired American executive, accomplished an astounding feat while golfing at The Baths — a ten-hole, par 3 course in Wisconsin — as part of the inaugural World's Longest Putt Competition he and some of his buddies organized. After two days putting for eight hours on end, trying to break the previous record, Stocki achieved greatness just as darkness descended. He drained a putt from 401 feet and two inches away to set the Guinness World Record. To put this putt into perspective: that stroke travelled close to 134 yards (the length of many par 3s) or more than one and a half times the distance from home plate to the centre field wall.

THE KEEPER OF THE GREENS

On the earliest courses, livestock like sheep grazed on the links, eating the grass from the tee to the green to keep its length in check. Rabbits, which have smaller teeth than sheep, nibbled away at the grass closer to the hole, which is why the earliest greens featured a surface with finer grass, more suitable for putting. During the hot summer months in Scotland, when the grass grew too rapidly for the grazing sheep to keep it under control, men with scythes were called in to cut the turf.

Over time, the care of fairways and greens was taken over more and more by people employed by golf clubs. Many of the earliest greenskeepers were also caddies and, like today, these men were jacks of all trades; when not carrying golfers' clubs, they used knives to cut out the holes, they set out flags, and they did what was necessary to make the ground smoother. For that task, their rudimentary tools were a wheelbarrow and a shovel or spade. To further improve and smooth the greens, these early greenskeepers used wooden hand rollers, birch brooms, and scythes.

As golf evolved, so did the maintenance equipment and the expectations of golfers. There are now college and university turf grass management programs devoted to this vocation, and modern greenskeepers (now usually called golf course superintendents) are required to know a lot more than just how to cut grass. They need to identify and understand the best way to treat turf grass diseases and do their part for the environment — finding ways to constantly reduce water usage while still keeping their courses green.

THE GREATEST UPSET IN GOLF HISTORY

The movie *The Greatest Game Ever Played*, based on Mark Frost's novel of the same name, was released in 2005. It tells the story of the 1913 U.S. Open at the Country Club in Brookline, Massachusetts, and Francis Ouimet — a twenty-year-old, self-taught amateur who had grown up across the street from the course. An underdog, he triumphed in an era when golf was played by the elites and a pair of Brits, Harry Vardon and Ted Ray, were the superstars of the day.

In order to play in the tournament, Ouimet had to negotiate time off his full-time job at a Boston sporting goods store. His caddie was a ten-year-old boy! The first day of the tournament included thirty-six holes. Ouimet was tied for seventeenth after the first round but only four strokes behind Vardon after the completion of the second eighteen holes. In the third round, Ouimet caught fire. He sank a par putt on the final hole, giving him the lowest score in the round, leaving him tied for the lead with Vardon, the four-time British Open winner, and Ray. The stage was set for the final eighteen holes.

Word of Ouimet's accomplishments reached downtown Boston, and people left work early and crowded onto streetcars to head to Brookline and catch a glimpse of this local boy wonder. A story about the match appeared on the front page of the *New York Times*, rare for a sports event. It was more than just the story of an underdog triumphing against the odds; it was seen as a triumph of America's egalitarian ideals over the privileged class system of England.

The next day the trio returned to The Country Club for an eighteen-hole playoff on Saturday, September 20, 1913. The crowds were estimated to be at least ten thousand strong, the largest gallery ever to watch a golf match to that point.

Ouimet won the final round, becoming the first amateur — and only the second American at the time — to win the U.S. Open. With local caddie Eddie Lowery, only ten years old, cheering him on from inside the ropes with repeated mantras like "keep your head down and keep your eye on the ball," Ouimet secured his win with a bogey-free back nine to shoot one-under 72, besting Vardon by five shots and Ray by six.

The significance of his win at Brookline reverberated far beyond Massachusetts. The news of this upset — a feel-good story of a working-class amateur David defeating Goliath — spawned an explosive growth in the game throughout North America. Golf became popular with the middle class and the working class, not something just played by the elite. According to the Francis Ouimet Scholarship Fund (founded in 1949 to assist students involved in the golfing community pay for college), the number of Americans playing golf soared from 350,000 in 1913 to 2.1 million a decade later, and the number of courses tripled during that time period.

A GOOD WALK SPOILED

The oft-quoted description of golf as "a good walk spoiled" holds true — at least in my opinion — when we consider the influence of the golf cart on the game. The stereotypical image of the modern golfer is an overweight man slumped in a golf cart, beer in one hand, cigar in the other, waiting to tee off. It's hard to imagine that when the first golf carts were introduced, you needed a doctor's prescription to use one.

Wonder when, why, and how the modern golf cart became a billion-dollar business and a revenue stream that golf course operators rely on to turn a profit?

Lyman Beecher, a retired electrical engineer and avid golfer from Clearwater, Florida, suffered from a disability preventing him from walking long distances. So, in 1932 he developed the first rudimentary golf cart to make it easier for him navigate golf courses. The three-wheeled vehicle, which looked more like a rickshaw was first used at Biltmore Forest Country Club in Asheville, North Carolina. The high cost of this electric-powered vehicle prohibited extensive use for many years.

In the 1950s, Texas oilman R.J. Jackson designed and received a patent for the first gas-powered golf cart, which was sold initially only by mail order. Jackson suffered from arthritis and the cart was dubbed the "Arthritis Special." Mainly due to the noise and the smoke from Jackson's gas-guzzling polluter, golf course owners resisted allowing them on their courses. Still, Jackson's invention sparked a great deal of interest in the possibilities of the machine. From the 1950s to the 1970s, many manufacturers improved upon his original idea, and before long, golf carts were being mass-produced and golf courses throughout North America were leasing fleets of them.

There are countless styles and models of carts now available. If you're looking to upscale your ride, you can buy carts modelled after luxury vehicles like the Cadillac Escalade, the Hummer, Rolls-Royce, and Bentley.

Many modern courses require players to use a golf cart, especially if walking long distances between holes would slow the pace of play. Non-players are now buying golf carts for use as a second vehicle, puttering around on them in retirement communities, on ranches, or in small towns.

An interesting note: the PGA Tour believes in the integrity of the game and the tradition of the players walking while caddies carry their bags. Carts are not allowed in tournaments. In a famous case, Casey Martin, who was born with a circulatory disorder in one leg, sued the PGA Tour for denying his use of a motorized golf cart during his one year on the game's top tour. Casey took the case all the way to the Supreme Court and won. Ironic that golf carts were first invented to allow those with disabilities to enjoy the game, but the use of a cart by a golfer with a disability was denied by one of the game's biggest influencers.

77

FOR LADIES ONLY

I started golfing when women were
supposed to know more about a cook
stove than a niblick.
— Ada Mackenzie, member,
Golf Canada Hall of Fame

All sports have a well-documented history of mis-
ogyny; golf is no exception. In the early years of the twentieth century, discrimination against women, whether in
the workforce or on the golf course, was the norm. Women
faced a different set of rules, all of which were written by
men. Ada Mackenzie suffered under those rules like all the
women of her time. She worked at a bank during the week,

so, as was true for most during these pioneering days of the sport, weekends were the only time to enjoy this popular pastime. Unfortunately, both of the private clubs she belonged to (the Mississauga Golf and Country Club and the Toronto Golf Club), allowed women to play only in the afternoon on Saturday and Sunday. The morning tee times were reserved for men. Since she could not own shares or vote, there was no opportunity for her to change those rules.

She came up with an idea of how to change things after a trip across the Atlantic Ocean. In 1921 she played in the Ladies' British Open Amateur Championship (now known as the Women's Amateur Championship). While in Britain, she learned of the existence of women-only clubs in Scotland: the Aberdeen Ladies Golf Club and Lundin Ladies Golf Club. They inspired her.

If you build it, she will come. This tweak of the memorable line from the classic 1989 baseball movie *Field of Dreams* sums up Mackenzie's vision. She decided that the only way women were going to be able to have full access to a golf course was to build one that catered specifically to them.

Before finding the perfect site that became the home of the Ladies' Golf Club of Toronto, Mackenzie visited more than twenty properties. Most of these were close to railway lines, since not many women drove cars at the time. Famous Canadian golf course architect Stanley Thompson, posing as Mackenzie's husband, joined the trailblazer on these site visits. This little white lie was necessary, she later explained to *Golf Digest*: "I posed as the wife of a man who was looking for a farm. If I had said I was looking for a ladies' golf course site, I might still be looking!"

The site that she finally found for the eighteen-hole course came complete with a three-and-a-half-storey home and a barn. Mackenzie convinced the lawyer who owned the property to sell it to her for $85,000. To secure financing (a down payment of $30,000 within three months was required to complete the sale), Mackenzie sold forty bonds at $1,000 each with 6 percent annual interest. She then promised the shareholders that she would sell three hundred memberships at $100 per share to raise additional capital.

Early bond buyers included prominent Toronto society women like Lady Eaton (wife of Sir John Craig Eaton, president of the T. Eaton Company). Despite purchasing a bond himself, newspaper magnate Dick Southam doubted Mackenzie's chances of succeeding with this venture, famously saying: "You haven't a snowball's chance. There never were that many women in the world who could work together."

On November 13, 1924, the sale was finalized, though, and the charter for the first all-women's golf club (the Ladies' Golf and Tennis Club of Toronto Limited) in Canada was granted. From the start, Mackenzie said there would be a male golf superintendent, as women did not have the expertise yet in maintenance, but "land girls with experience driving tractors" would provide the daily upkeep of the course.

The first twenty years were a financial struggle for the Ladies', but they found ways to cut costs, to scrimp, and to save to continue operating. They proved that Southam and other doubters were wrong, and they did not have to resort to opening membership to men to remain in business, as did the Women's National Golf & Tennis Club on Long Island in New York. That club, which was founded in response to a local club in the area barring women from becoming members, survived as a women-only establishment only until the Second World War, when, ironically, the club merged with the same course that had previously not allowed women.

More than one hundred years since Mackenzie founded the Ladies' Golf Club of Toronto, it is the only remaining private club in North America established by women for women. Men are allowed to play as annual guest-card holders, but they can only play in off-peak hours (just as females were limited to doing at so many private clubs in the past — Mackenzie's initial inspiration), and they do not have a vote on any club affairs. Mackenzie's portrait hangs in the front hall of the clubhouse as a constant reminder of the power of women.

GREAT SCOT! BANISHMENT

In Shakespeare's *Macbeth*, Macduff is banished from his home of Scotland in act four, scene three, physically and mentally. While golfers were not banished — or exiled from their country for playing the pastime they invented — the game was briefly banned, not just once, but three times!

The first time occurred in 1457. Under the rule of James II, an act of Parliament was passed that not only banned golf, but also football. It read:

> Football and golf should be utterly condemned and stopped. And ... a pair of targets should be made up at all parish churches and shooting should be practised

each Sunday.... And concerning football and golf, we ordain that [those found playing these games] be punished by the local barons and, failing them, by the King's officers.

The ban was implemented for a couple of reasons: the threat of the English invading was ever present, and the king did not want his citizens distracted by any games. Rather than practising their pitches or their putts, he banned the sport to make sure they spent their leisure time practising their marksmanship; military training was compulsory for anyone over the age of twelve. Secondly, since both golf and football were often played in public places, not on formal courses or pitches (i.e., in the streets or churchyards), the royal government claimed these sports were dangerous and put other citizens at risk of getting hurt.

The Scottish Parliament repeated this ban in 1471 and 1491. The revised parliamentary act of 1491 referred to football and golf as "pointless sports," and stated that if citizens were caught playing one of these games, a fine of forty shillings would be collected by the sheriffs and bailiffs.

In a related story, final rounds of PGA Tour golf tournaments are played on Sundays; it's also a day many players enjoy a round. But skipping church and golfing on the sabbath, that was a sin, at least in 1604. The Reverend James Scott's minute book, which resides today in the National

Library of Scotland, spoke of this offence when he wrote about four youth "who were convicted of profaning the Lord's Sabbath by absenting themselves from hearing the Word, & playing at the Gowf in Time of Preaching."

Amen that wiser minds prevailed. For Sunday afternoons are perfect for communing with Mother Nature on a golf course somewhere or watching the final round of a PGA Tour event on TV and praying for your favourite player to win.

THE NUMBERS GAME

Sports are all about numbers. Baseball's rules stipulate the number of strikes and outs in an inning and the number of innings in a game; hockey has rules about the number of periods in a game; tennis has a rule about the number of sets in a game. Different sports declare how many points various actions — a touchdown in football, a basket in basketball — are worth. Golf is no different. But why eighteen holes?

The myth people love to tell is that there are eighteen holes because the Scots, who invented the game, decided to match the number of holes to the number of shots in a bottle of Scotch. Sounds plausible … but it's not. The real reason is not quite as appealing. It happened more as a result of the process of elimination. Many of the earliest links courses over the first century of the sport did not share the same number of holes. Usually, the number of holes simply depended on how much land was available.

In view of recent golf design trends of twelve-hole courses — and other multiples — it is interesting to learn that the first layout of the Old Course at St. Andrews featured twenty-two holes. Eventually, in 1764, St. Andrews set the modern standard of eighteen, when four of the shortest holes at the Old Course morphed into two (played in two directions with separate tees and greens). Still, other courses did not adopt the eighteen-hole course as a standard immediately. Prestwick Golf Club, the home of the first Open Championship, and designed by Old Tom Morris, was a twelve-hole course until it expanded to eighteen in 1882.

Eventually, the majority of courses in the United Kingdom — and later, as the sport expanded, the majority of courses in North America and other countries — simply copied St. Andrews, and eighteen holes became the global standard.

GOLF UNDER THE STARS

Most sports — from baseball and tennis to football and soccer — are played under the lights, and often at night, so why not golf? Well, for one, the playing field is a little larger — lighting an entire course is not as simple as adding some overhead stadium lights.

Still, despite the challenges and additional costs involved in equipping a course for golf under the lights, night golf is catching on. It is huge in South Korea, where it's called "white night" golf; South Korea is now the third-largest market for the sport in the world beyond the United States and Japan. Twenty percent of the courses in the republic now offer night golf. There is an undersupply of courses to satiate Koreans' demand to play (Seoul, a city of ten million people, has only one course and it's reserved for the military), so 117 of those offer tee times that start as late as 8:00 p.m. Some of the nine-hole courses also stay open past midnight.

This nocturnal variation of the sport is also gaining popularity in North America. In the United States, a growing number of courses, mostly nine-hole or shorter par 3 courses, offer a unique golf experience. (This addition, of course, provides another revenue stream for course operators.) The best part: you can fit that round in on your time. Night golf offers more flexibility, so you do not have to give up your Saturday morning or Sunday afternoon family time for a tee time. Night golf also has some drawbacks. Reading greens is tricky due to the artificial lighting and shadows, and those warm lights also attract more bugs.

GOLF IN THE LAND OF THE RISING SUN

Ready for a round of *gorufu*? That's Japanese for golf.

Englishman Arthur Groom established Japan's very first golf course in 1903. An avid outdoorsman, Groom built a cottage near the summit of Mount Rokko and was inspired to build a golf course on leased land on the slopes of the mountain not far from his home. Following three years of clearing rocks by hand, a four-hole loop was completed. By 1904, the course expanded to eighteen holes and a par 61. The Mount Rokko course is located on the flat top of the mountain one thousand metres above sea level, near the city of Kobe. This course, known now as the Kobe Golf Club, remains a popular place to play.

Until the Tokyo Golf Club was founded in 1913, all courses in Japan were created by expatriate residents of the country. The Tokyo Golf Club, which was founded by — and for — Japanese nationals, has played an integral role in the growth of the game in the country. It has moved sites a few times, from Komazawa to Asaka to Sayama on the outskirts of the Japanese capital and the world's most populous city, where it remains today. Following the founding of the Tokyo Golf Club, the game's popularity and the number of clubs grew. By 1941, there were twenty-three courses in Japan, but during the Second World War, most of these courses were expropriated by the Japanese military. Following the war, they were seized by the U.S. occupying forces for use as military bases or for agricultural production.

By 1952, as the foreign occupiers had left, courses started to return, and golf grew at a feverish pace. By 1956, there were seventy-two courses, and between 1960 and 1964, the number of courses increased from 195 to 424 — peaking in the early 1970s at more than one thousand courses. From 1964 to 1992, the number of Japanese who took to this sport grew from ten million to 102 million. The 1987 Act on Development of Specified Integrated Resort Districts, which reduced protections on agricultural lands and forest preserves, added to this building boom. Boasting 2,500, Japan is home to the second highest number of golf courses in the world, next only to the United States.

It's not a surprise that Japan has produced a number of world-class golfers. On the PGA Tour, Masashi Ozaki, known more familiarly by his nickname "Jumbo," was the first Japanese star. In 1989 Jumbo spent two hundred consecutive weeks in the top ten of the world golf rankings. In the twenty-first century, the modern Japanese golfing great is Hideki Matsuyama, who peaked at number two in the world rankings in 2017. On April 11, 2021, Matsuyama became the first Japanese player — and also the first Asian-born player — to win the Masters.

GOLF IN TIMES OF WAR

Even world wars and bombs falling from the air were not enough to put a halt to golf. It offered a temporary escape from the horrors and atrocities happening in Europe. In Canada, there was a golf boom during the First World War. Tournaments raised funds to support the war and politicians encouraged Canadians to get their dose of exercise on the links.

In England, golf courses were transformed and doubled as training grounds for military exercises; this is where many Canadians discovered this sport for the first time.

Oh, and not surprisingly, golf during times of war had some temporary rules like these seven adopted in 1941 by Richmond Golf Club in London, England. Hard to fathom in the twenty-first century, but they illustrate the lengths clubs and citizens went to keep some semblance of normality and still enjoy their favourite pastime:

- Players are asked to collect the bomb and shrapnel splinters to save these causing damage to the mowing machines.
- In competitions, during gunfire or while bombs are falling, players may take shelter without penalty or ceasing play.
- The positions of known delayed-action bombs are marked by red flags at a reasonable, but not guaranteed, safe distance therefrom.
- Shrapnel and/or bomb splinters on the Fairway, or in Bunkers, within a club's length of a ball, may be moved without penalty, and no penalty shall be incurred if a ball is thereby caused to move accidentally.
- A ball moved by enemy action may be replaced, or if lost, or destroyed, a ball may be dropped not nearer the hole without penalty.
- A ball lying in a crater may be lifted and dropped not nearer the hole, preserving the line to the hole, without penalty.
- A player whose stroke is affected by the simultaneous explosion of a bomb may play another ball. Penalty one stroke.

BING AND THE CROSBY CLAMBAKE

One of the longest-running tournaments on the PGA Tour, the AT&T National Pebble Beach Pro-Am was started by crooner and Hollywood hobnobber Bing Crosby.

Crosby was one of the biggest stars of his generation, known particularly for his silky-smooth voice. He was also a passionate golfer. In 1937 he decided to start his own tournament and put up the initial prize purse of $3,000. The idea: organize a fun tournament with his Hollywood friends in a team format of professionals and amateurs, and then when the golf was done, enjoy a clambake together.

The inaugural event took place at Rancho Santa Fe Country Club in San Diego, California, where Crosby was a member, and near where he lived. Sam Snead was the first victor, winning $500. Following the tournament, Crosby hosted a party at his home. That first thirty-six-hole affair was a hit, and the tournament gradually grew from there. In 1947 Crosby relocated the tournament to the Monterey Peninsula, and it became an official PGA Tour event that continues today. Up until 1967, the first three rounds were contested at Cypress Point Club and Monterey Peninsula Country Club before moving to Pebble Beach for the final round.

The pro-am part of this tournament, which still continues today, featured celebrities from pro athletes to actors. Crosby's list of A-list friends from Hollywood was endless, so the field always featured the top stars of the day. In later years, Bill Murray was a fixture of the event from 1993 to 2023, adding comedic relief on the fairways. Today, nearly every PGA and LPGA Tour tournament features a pro-am on the day before the first round begins. These events raise money for local charities.

What started more as a schmooze-fest for bon vivant Crosby — an excuse to gather friends together for a couple of days of fun, games, and food, and an opportunity to learn a few tips from golf professionals in the process — ended up driving the growth of the sport's popularity. For nearly eighty years, Bing's big little idea has brought tourism dollars each January to the Monterey Peninsula.

84 GOLF ETIQUETTE

No other sport is defined as much by its unofficial etiquette as its official rules. Etiquette is really the heart of golf, and it is because of this that many laud it as a sport that teaches you about life and how to be a better person.

You have to keep your own score: that teaches honesty. The player who wins the previous hole always gets to tee first on the next hole. That teaches honour. Pace of play is all about respect and humility. If you or your group is playing too slow, and the group behind is always waiting, the common courtesy is to let the group play through; it's not about your pride. How the dress code of the sport evolved is also about etiquette — making the right impression and showing respect to the club where you play and to your fellow players. Simple things like tucking in your shirt and wearing your hat forward, not backward. Finally, taking care of the golf course and leaving it the way you found it or would like others to leave it for you — by fixing your divots and raking bunkers — is about respecting the course.

THE BLOCK PARTY

The 105th playing of the PGA Championship occurred at historic Oak Hill Country Club in Rochester, New York, on a late May weekend in 2023. The tournament is now remembered more because of the man who finished tied for fifteenth than because of the winner who collected his third Wanamaker Trophy. While Brooks Koepka was the victor, the storyline of this week belonged to a California club professional named Michael Block.

Just like John Daly at this same major in 1991, Block became a household name overnight, and an underdog who fans flocked to and became inspired by. In his press conference following the final round, Block even alluded to that other blue-collar hero when a reporter asked why his story resonated with so many people: "I'm like the new John

Daly, but I don't have a mullet, and I'm not quite as big as him yet."

This "Oak Hill Cinderella Man" was the only one of twenty other PGA Club professionals who even made the cut. The chants on Sunday from outside the ropes were deafening: "Block. Block. Block." The forty-six-year-old finished with a one over par in the final round to finish T15 for the major. Not bad for a golf pro who had never made the cut in his previous four times playing this event. Block, who normally taught lessons for $150 per hour, earned a cool $288,333 at Oak Hill. He went from being a PGA teaching professional to being a household name and sports celebrity. He was offered exemptions to play in several more PGA Tour events, which he did and enjoyed the fame while it lasted.

As if Block's fairy tale week in Rochester could get any better, in the final round, paired with Rory McIlroy, on the par 3 fifteenth, 151-yard hole, Block dunked his tee shot on the fly for a hole-in-one. Block did not even know it went in and kept asking McIlroy what happened as the pair started down the fairway. McIlroy, walking a little farther ahead, was the first to learn that the ball had gone in. Immediately, he strutted back down the fairway to give Block a huge hug, apparently telling him five times the ball was in the hole before Block believed him. In his post-round press conference, the club presented him with the flag from the fifteenth hole as a souvenir of this incredible feat.

From teaching lessons for $150 an hour at Arroyo Trabuco Golf Club in Mission Viejo, California, to cashing a cheque for a week's work for just shy of $300,000. Not bad, Mr. Block. Not too bad.

86

CALIFORNIA DREAMIN'

Amateur golfers competing in professional golf events is nothing new. Every year, the Masters invites the winners of the U.S. Amateur, British Amateur, Latin American Amateur, and U.S. Mid-Amateur to play. But for one of those players to win — beating golfers that are paid to put that little white ball in a hole week after week for a living — is rare. In the history of the game, only eight players have accomplished this feat.

The first time it happened was 1945 at the North and South Open when Cary Middlecoff bettered the pros, besting professional Denny Shute by five strokes. That same year Fred Haas won the Memphis Invitational. Frank Stranahan, who received instruction as a junior from Byron Nelson, is the only player in the history of the PGA Tour to win more than once as an amateur — doing it four times from 1945 to 1948 (Durham Open, Kansas City Invitational Victory Bond Golf Tournament, the Fort Worth Invitational, and the Miami Open). The other amateurs who beat the pros include Doug Sanders (1956 Canadian Open); Scott Verplank (1985 Western Open); and Phil Mickelson (1991 Northern Telecom Open).

The most recent, and one of the most dramatic, amateur victories came in 2024 when Nick Dunlap did some California dreaming to win the American Express tournament on the PGA Tour. The twenty-year-old came to the tournament as the reigning U.S. Amateur champion. He was the only non-professional in the 156-player field. In the third round, the sophomore at the University of Alabama shot a twelve-under 60 to enter the final round with a three-shot lead. A par putt on the final hole Sunday gave Dunlap a final score of twenty-nine under 259, which broke the tournament scoring record, and sealed this unbelievable victory. An interesting thing to note: PGA Tour rules do not allow amateurs to win money, so the $1.5 million first prize went to the second-place finisher. After a lot of thinking, less than one week later, the collegian announced he was turning pro and would join the PGA Tour full-time. When Dunlap won his second Tour event, and first as a professional, (the Barracuda Championship) later that season, he received $720,000.

HOW LOW CAN YOU GO?

Most golfers are lucky to break 60 for nine holes the first time they tee it up — the average golf score is somewhere in the fifties. So, imagine shooting below 60 for eighteen holes. With the advancements in both club and ball technology, modern pro golfers regularly shoot in the sixties, but breaking that magic number is rare.

From 2016 to 2024, the professional PGA Tour–sanctioned event record was 58, co-held by Jim Furyk, (at the 2016 Travelers) and Stephen Jaeger (at the 2016 Ellie Mae Classic). In February 2024, that record was broken. A new record for lowest score was set in Bogota, Colombia, when Christobal Del Solar posted a 57 in a Korn Ferry event[*]

---

[*] The Korn Ferry Tour is the developmental tour of the PGA Tour; it features golfers who have not yet qualified for the latter tour and those who qualified but did not earn enough points to stay on the tour.

at El Country Club's Paco Course. The Chilean shot 27 (eight under) on the front nine and 30 on the back nine. In this record-setting performance, he hit all eighteen greens in regulation and took only twenty-seven putts.

Outside of the professional ranks, according to the *Guinness Book of World Records*, the lowest eighteen-hole golf score ever recorded is a 55 (sixteen under par) shot by Australian Rhein Gibson at River Oaks Golf Club in Edmond, Oklahoma, on May 12, 2012. The round included two eagles, twelve birdies, and four pars.

THE WORLD'S WORST GOLFER

Imagine watching professional golf for the first time on TV and thinking, *I can do that!* Well, that's exactly what Maurice Flitcroft, a crane operator in his mid-forties, was inspired to do by his first glimpses of this sport on the TV. So, he decided to give golf a try. If Flitcroft, like most beginners, had just bought a set of clubs and signed up for a few lessons at his local course, that would have been the end of this story; it sure would not be fascinating. But this Englishman took it quite a few steps further.

After ordering a half-set of clubs in the mail, Flitcroft studied some golf instruction manuals he found in his local library and practised what he learned from those books on a nearby beach. Then, he registered to play in the local qualifier for the British Open Championship. How did he register without an official handicap, which all amateur golfers are required to provide? The dupester signed up as a professional, and no one bothered to confirm his claims until it was too late!

Flitcroft shot 121 — forty-nine over par — in the first round, the highest score ever posted in any part of the Open. While golf fans and newspapers were intrigued by Flitcroft's story, the R&A was livid at this embarrassing display in the world's oldest major. They banned him for life from playing in any Open qualifier.

This ban did not stop the prankster. Two years later, posing as an American, using a ridiculous pseudonym (Gene Paychecki), and sporting a goofy disguise, he weaselled his way into another qualifier. He managed to get in a few holes before the R&A caught on to his act. Undeterred, the Englishman tried a couple of more times to fool the British bureaucrats. The first time was in 1983, when he posed as a golfer from Switzerland named Gerald Hoppy; the final time was in 1990, when he adopted the nom du plume James Beau Jolley.

The press dubbed the hero of the people the "world's worst golfer." By the 1980s, his exploits were so well known in the United Kingdom that they became part of the British golf lexicon. The term "a Flitcroft" is used for a hacker or hopeless golfer. The simpleton was even admired in America, where clubs named trophies and tournaments in his honour. In 1988 a course in Grand Rapids, Michigan (Blythefield Country Club), even flew Flitcroft and his family overseas for its annual "Maurice Gerald Flitcroft Member-Guest Tournament."

This golfer's story was told in a book published in 2010, *The Phantom of the Open*, which was later adapted into a movie of the same name in 2022. A folk hero to some, a menace and embarrassment to the golf establishment, Flitcroft passed away March 24, 2007, aged seventy-seven.

89 UNIQUE SHORT COURSES

I've long felt eighteen holes is too many. By the time I hit the twelfth hole, I've had enough. I'm not tired physically, but mentally I'm spent. For the final six holes, my focus usually wanes, and my play reflects this mental fatigue. For the record, I'm far from the only one who feels this way. Starting in the 2000s, as golf's popularity dipped, one suggestion to "grow the game," made by Jack Nicklaus and other leaders of the game, was to build courses with different routings of, say, ten or twelve holes — anything less than the standard eighteen. Shortening courses would counter one of the reasons many never play the game: the amount of time it takes to complete.

The irony is, before eighteen holes was adopted by the game's governing bodies as the official length for tournament games, many of the earliest links courses had different lengths. Some had more holes and many had less than this norm.

Today, there are four-hole courses, ten-hole courses, and even one with twenty-one! Here are a few examples of some fun shorter courses designed in recent years in an attempt to attract new players to this grand old game.

The Oregon mecca, Bandon Dunes Golf Resort, which opened its first course in 1999, now features six distinct links courses, all modelled after the style of the earliest Scottish layouts. One of these, Bandon Preserve, is a fun thirteen-hole, par 3 course, whose holes range in length from sixty-three yards to 150 yards — the Pacific Ocean provides the backdrop for every hole. Another par 3 is called Shorty's (after the late early caretaker and pioneer of this property, Shorty Dow); it features nineteen holes. It's not officially a "shorter" course, but it is a good example of how different combinations of holes are becoming more popular.

One of the three courses at Sand Valley Resort in Wisconsin — the Sandbox — is a seventeen-hole short course.

Forest Dunes, in northern Michigan, offers a ten-hole, par 3 course. This golf resort also features a unique course, designed by American architect Tom Doak. Called the Loop, this innovative reversible course layout is played in two directions. The black routing is played in a clockwise rotation one day; the red routing is played in a counter-clockwise manner the next day. There are no defined tee boxes that golfers are used to; an area that serves as a tee box one day may become part of the fairway when the course is played in the opposite direction.

At QuickSands at Gamble Sands in Washington State, four hours from Seattle, there is another course with a non-traditional routing. This short course has a fourteen-hole, par 3 layout. The names of holes — Plinko, Donut, and Boomerang are a few — show that the course is all about fun. The golf experience is livened up with a mix of classic rock and today's pop and hip-hop hits that blast from a course-wide sound system.

In the land where golf was invented, one of the coolest courses with fewer than eighteen holes is the Shiskine Golf and Tennis Club. On the Ayrshire coast of Scotland, it has been dubbed as the "greatest 12-hole course in the world."

The course opened in 1896 with nine holes and expanded to eighteen, but during the Second World War, six holes were converted to agricultural land, leaving the current twelve-hole layout. There are other legacies of those earlier times; for example, if the pro shop is closed upon your arrival, there is an "Honesty Box" slot to pay your green fees.

A final short course that offers a unique golf experience is the Horse Course at the Prairie Club — a resort property tucked into Nebraska's sandhills. Designed by Gil Hanse and Geoff Shackelford, what sets this 10-hole layout apart from other courses featuring less than eighteen holes is that there is no one way to play. The name alludes to the playground basketball game of H.O.R.S.E., which involves players trying to emulate their opponents' feats. A player that fails to succeed gets a letter. In a similar fashion, the games at the Horse showcase the creativity of the players. There are no tee boxes — the winner of the previous hole decides where the next shot will be from — and they pick which green will be used for the hole. No one keeps score in these games; players just enjoy a fun series of individual hole matches.

A PLUGGED BUNKER SHOT TO REMEMBER

For the Fords, golf was a family affair. Doug Ford Sr. (no relation to the Ontario premier) was a golf professional, as were three of his uncles. And both of Ford's sons (Doug Jr. and Mike) also became golf professionals.

Ford is remembered as a player who did not waste time. One scribe said he "plays like a racehorse"; another said, "he goes around the course in Mach One." With this aggressive approach to the game, Ford had an uncanny ability to win. He won nineteen times in the 1950s. Fourteen of his wins were on the PGA Tour. They included the PGA Championship in 1955, which he won on his first try, and the Masters in 1957.

Ford's Augusta finish is a golf story worth retelling. While the final round leader, Sam Snead, faltered several holes behind him, Ford went for broke. The first bold move came on the par 5 fifteenth fairway, when he ignored his caddie's plea to use a 4-iron to lay up on his second shot and avoid landing in the water. Ford was in the mood for taking a risk, though. He turned to his caddie and said, "I'm no good at playing it safe." Instead of using the iron, he grabbed his spoon (a hickory-shafted club equivalent to today's 5-wood). Barely clearing the water, the drive somehow landed on the edge of the green. His gamble paid off. Ford putt two for a birdie.

But that was not what Ford would call "the greatest shot he ever played." That came on the par 4 eighteenth hole, when his approach to the green landed short and got plugged in the bunker. Using a sand wedge, he miraculously managed to dig the ball out and onto the green, where it proceeded to roll into the hole. With this stupendous shot, he finished with a birdie and a final round score of 66 to beat Snead by three strokes. Interviewed in 2010, for a *Golf Digest* "My Shot" feature, Ford shared that in executing this plugged sand shot, he relied on teachings from his misspent youth in Manhattan pool rooms. (One of Ford's uncles was a New York state billiard champion.) Doug relied on his natural feel for angles learned from playing billiards.

More than five decades after this heroic shot at Augusta, Ford often sat in his golf cart, twirling that famous wedge in his hands, as he watched son Doug give playing lessons to snowbirds at the Florida course where he played while wintering in the state.

GRIP IT AND RIP IT!

The saying "grip it and rip it" refers to the unleash-ing of the power of your driver by grasping it tightly and smashing a drive into the stratosphere. Smashing a drive gives one the same feeling as hitting a home run in base-ball. Modern advances in technology have resulted in huge improvement to both equipment and balls, and so even the average hacker is able to hit a ball more than three hundred yards.

So, what is the longest drive ever achieved in a profes-sional competition? That happened, albeit with a fifty-five kilometre-per-hour tailwind, at the Winterwood Golf Club in Las Vegas in 1974, when a sixty-four-year-old named Mike Austin, playing in the U.S. National Seniors Tournament, hit a drive (using a persimmon club) 515 yards.

A ROYAL FIRST IN MONTREAL

In 1873 golf history was made in Montreal when eight gentlemen, led by Scotsman Alexander Dennistoun, introduced the "royal and ancient game" to the Americas by founding the Montreal Golf Club. It should be noted that these trailblazers were not actually the first ones to play golf in Canada. According to a report from the *Montreal Herald*, dated December 25, 1826, a group of Scottish immigrants gathered at Priest's Farm just outside the city to play a game. This is the first recorded instance of golf being played in this country.

The course, which is ranked one of the top in Canada, was initially located on Fletcher's Fields (now Jeanne-Mance Park) on the outskirts of Mount Royal Park; since then, it has moved locations twice. Eleven years after its founding, Queen Victoria granted the club permission to add the title "Royal" to its name. This private club is one of approximately seventy worldwide (most of which are found in the United Kingdom and former British colonies) that have received the Crown's permission to call themselves "Royal." According to Scott Macpherson's book *Golf's Royal Clubs*, this practice started in 1833 when the captain of the Perth Golfing Society asked King William IV if the club could call itself the Royal Perth; the English monarch agreed. The way a club goes about requesting this royal stamp of approval hasn't changed: the club submits a formal application, and the reigning monarch always has the final say.

The Royal Montreal Golf Club can lay claim to a number of other firsts. It hosted the first Canadian Open, in 1904, and since then, it has held nine other Canadian Opens and two Presidents Cup (2007 and 2024) matches.

Mrs. William Wallace Watson (née Florence Stancliffe) was the first woman to join the club, and when she was elected to the board in 1891, she became the first female board member of any golf club in North America. An interesting aside: she was also one of the 1,195 passengers of the RMS *Lusitania* that perished on May 7, 1915, when a German submarine sank the British ocean liner. The Royal has promoted women in golf in other ways too. In 1901 the club held the inaugural Canadian Women's Amateur.

L.A. CONFIDENTIAL

In 2023 the world was finally given a peek inside one of the most mysterious and mythic Hollywood golf grounds when the Los Angeles Country Club hosted the 123rd U.S. Open. Sportswriter Sam Farmer, in the *Los Angeles Times*, called the Los Angeles Country Club "the greatest course people have never seen." That anonymity is exactly what members of this toney private club want. The course is *very* private and *very* exclusive — you might say it discriminates.

Getting an invite to join this swanky club is about who you know — and more importantly who likes you. The members (numbering around eight hundred) have always been very particular. For example, they have always held a disdain for actors and entertainers — Bing Crosby, Groucho

Marx, and Hugh Hefner were all denied membership. (This Hollywood crowd are more welcome at Riviera Country Club or Bel-Air Country Club.) Connections are important, but wealth is necessary too, if you want to become a member. It is rumoured a membership at L.A. Country Club costs $250,000, and that is just the initiation fee.

Most Hollywood golf and country clubs were founded in the Roaring Twenties. L.A. Country Club's history dates back further. The first iteration was called the Los Angeles Golf Club. A group of Angelenos leased a sixteen-acre property and laid out a nine-hole course. The club moved a couple of times before settling on its current location at 10101 Wilshire Blvd. Los Angeles grew and expanded around this enclave; the more than 320-acre property is now estimated to be worth $8 billion.

THE WEDGE MAN

The moral of this story: always raise your hand.
That simple action led to Canadian Bob Vokey designing
some of the most popular wedges in golf, wedges with the
most forgiving grinds.[*]

Born in Montreal, Quebec, Vokey learned the basics
of his trade from his father, a tool and die maker. During
informal summer apprenticeships, Vokey soaked up the science and the craft of his father's trade — he learned how
to measure angles and mastered the operating of grinders
and lathes. He later transferred and adapted these skills to
modifying his golf clubs.

---

[*] Grind refers to the geometry of the sole of a wedge. The manipulation or re-
moval of material from the sole will give the club more or less bounce and
improve consistent contact with the turf.

Flash forward to December 1966. Vokey arrived in the United States with professional dreams. He quickly realized that his destiny lay not in competing, but instead in using his skills to craft game-changing clubs. In his first small shop, called Bob's Custom Golf Shop, in Fallbrook, California, he began modifying clubs for customers. His reputation grew by word of mouth; Vokey's next venture was the Golf Master. There, he started to build and repair clubs for the professional staff in La Costa Golf Course in Carlsbad, California.

By 1986 TaylorMade came calling. Vokey started building clubs for them exclusively. Five years later, he helped launch the Founders Club, a company specializing in metal woods and irons. Finally, in 1996, he realized his true calling as a master wedge maker while working at Titleist. That day, the president, Steve Pelisek, stood in a room full of employees and shared his goal of increasing the brand's market share in the wedge category. He asked for volunteers to take on this challenge. Vokey immediately shot up his hand.

Designing wedges, for Vokey, was a new endeavour. Previously, he had focused mostly on designing woods, but he was always fascinated by the intricacies of wedges and how essential they were for amateurs and professionals. Vokey was confident he could build a better wedge. As Pelisek recalls, the morning following this staff meeting, he discovered Bob's office was already filled with hundreds of wedges. The master craftsman had his head down and was already lost in the work of designing a wedge that would become the go-to short-game weapon for both pros and amateurs.

Vokey spent hundreds of hours fine-tuning designs and using the grind wheel to produce a product he believed in. He spent eight months going from tournament to tournament on the PGA Tour. His Titleist bag was stuffed with prototypes that he asked players to test and give feedback on.

Vokey believes that one size or design does not fit all, so he designs his wedges based on a player's likes and needs. Dozens of PGA Tour pros have admitted that the wedges that Vokey designed for them helped them win tournaments.

One day in 1997, at the St. Jude Classic in Memphis, Tennessee, eleven-time PGA Tour winner Andy Bean tried one of Vokey's fifty-six-degree sand wedge prototypes during practice before his round. From the first swing, Bean felt connected to the club. He sank a few chips at the practice green and snuggled some sand shots right up to the cup. Bean, with Vokey's permission, added the club to his bag for the tournament. He never returned the club, telling the craftsman, "Since you're such a good club maker, you can make another one of these!" Bean continued to use this club until the ridges almost disappeared.

A fascinating footnote: twenty years after Bean "borrowed" this wedge, Meggan Gardner, director of Heritage Services at Golf Canada, received an unexpected call from the retired pro. Bean asked, "Would the Canadian Golf Hall of Fame like the very first Vokey wedge ever used on the PGA Tour?"

Of course, Gardner replied yes.

Now this piece of golf history is preserved as part of Vokey's legacy. More than eleven million Vokey wedges later, the master craftsman is a member of the Canadian Golf Hall of Fame.

95

TAKE ME FOR A LOOP

Can I carry your clubs? This question is uttered by caddies at golf courses around the globe. Many North American teenagers have earned — or will earn — their first wages as caddies at private golf clubs. Where did this noun come from and how did caddying become a part of the professional game and adopted practice at some private golf clubs?

Caddie derives from the French word "*le cadet,*" which means "the youngest member of a family." The Scots adopted many French words, and this is one of them. Early on there were many different spellings of this word (cady, caddy, cadie or caddie), but they all referred to an errand boy. Eventually, the use of this term narrowed. Originally, the label was given to a general porter who was hired for a variety of odd jobs; today, it is used exclusively for a person who carries a golfer's clubs and offers help during a round.

In the early days, there were no golf bags, and as paintings from the time show, caddies just carried the bundle of clubs in their arms. The earliest caddies at St. Andrews and other links courses in Scotland were semi-professionals, and many others also worked as part of the course maintenance crews.

In the United States, caddies became popular, and many courses employed a caddie corps at the ready in a specially designed area of the course called the caddie yard. The invention of golf carts (see story 76) contributed to a decline in the use and need for these helpers. As more players chose to ride in a golf cart, the tradition of someone else carrying their clubs has become increasingly obsolete. Still, many private clubs keep this tradition alive. Employing caddies not only provides jobs to younger members of the community, it also helps introduce the game to children from lower-income backgrounds who might not otherwise ever step foot on a golf course.

This tradition also remains on the professional tours, where caddies and players form bonds. Part psychologist, caddies offer advice to their players and cheer them up when they've made a bad shot. (They sometimes become the player's punching bag, taking the blame for a player's mistake.) Caddies are also strategic advisors: they help PGA Tour pros whose bags they carry figure out the exact yardage of each shot so that the players can determine the right club to hit.

Professional caddies, if they pick up a loop for one of the top players, can earn a fine living. Some even become celebrities in their own right, almost as well known as the players for whom they caddie. A few have been given nicknames, such as Bones, Killer, and Fluff. Their pay varies, but on the PGA Tour, most caddies earn a weekly salary along with a percentage of the player's earnings. That base pay ranges from $1,500 to $3,000 weekly, but caddies can earn up to 10 percent of their player's winnings, which can add a pretty tidy bonus if their player consistently plays well. Tour caddies also can earn extra money by signing sponsorship agreements to wear a brand's hat or its logo on their shirtsleeve. To illustrate this earning potential, it's estimated Justin Thomas's former caddie, Jim "Bones" Mackay, made more than half a million in 2021. No surprise, the caddie who has earned the most all-time is Steve Williams, who was Tiger Woods's long-time looper; it's believed Williams earned more than $12 million caddying for Tiger.

THE MAKING OF THE MOST AUTHENTIC GOLF MOVIE

Sports movies, when done well, are usually comed-ic (*Bull Durham*) or heart-warming (*Hoosiers*). Golf as a subject for feature films dates as far back as the romantic comedy *Spring Fever*, released in 1927. Since then, Hollywood has used the sport as the focus for many movies, some more memorable than others. For laughs, nothing beats the 1980s slapstick *Caddyshack*, which took place at the fictional Bushwood Country Club. The movie satirized life inside the gates of one of these private playgrounds for the rich and featured some of the funniest men of their generation: Chevy Chase, Rodney Dangerfield, and Bill Murray.

But when it comes to one of the most authentic golf films ever made, the vote goes to *Tin Cup* (1996). No happy

Hollywood ending here. Instead, the climax sees the movie's main character — underdog, washed-up club professional Roy McAvoy (played by Kevin Costner) — blow the chance to win the U.S. Open. Up by two shots, McAvoy makes a bad decision and ends up recording a twelve on the final hole to lose. McAvoy was too proud to "lay up," (i.e., he possessed an aggressive mindset that did not allow him to ever consider a safer, more strategic shot). Instead, he lived by the motto, "Go for broke!"

This fictional character's collapse has now become part of golf lingo. Anytime a player, whether a professional in a high-stakes tournament or an amateur in a game with their buddies on a Saturday afternoon, makes a dumb decision and loses a tournament or match, people call it a "Tin Cup moment."

Tin Cup opened number one at the box office and earned $76 million, exceeding the film's budget by about $30 million.

A few other fun and fascinating facts about this golf movie that helped make it the most authentic portrayal of the sport ever on the big screen:

- Gary McCord, the American golf professional and TV commentator, was hired as a golf consultant to work with Kevin Costner, who did not want a stunt double and insisted on hitting all his own shots. McCord demanded and got paid $250,000. To earn that lofty fee, he, of course, instructed Costner on the use of the different clubs and on the swing. He also taught the actor about how golfers win — and lose. To illustrate the latter, McCord shared some of his most famous meltdowns on the golf course (like the time he made a sixteen at Colonial Country Club that included hitting five balls into the water).

- A TV tower was constructed to replicate the actual structures seen at all televised PGA Tour events.
- Actual sponsors were signed for all the fictional golfers in the movie.
- The driving range where McAvoy worked teaching before playing on the pro circuit was built from scratch in a remote spot an hour south of Tucson, Arizona.
- United States Golf Association officials were hired to review the courses used in the film and make sure they were in real U.S. Open condition.

GOLF BY DESIGN

Old Tom Morris is not only considered the first greenskeeper, but he is also considered the first golf course designer. Before the beginning of the twentieth century, there was no such profession as golf course architect.

What is known today as the golden age of golf course architecture occurred when the sport exploded in North America. This period was fuelled by the upset win by amateur Francis Ouimet over Brits Harry Vardon and Ted Ray in the 1913 U.S. Open (see story 75). In the golf craze that followed, courses were built all over the United States. The number of golf courses in the United States grew from fewer than 750 in 1916 to nearly six thousand by 1930. The affluence of the Roaring Twenties offered the perfect economic environment for the growth of the sport.

Designers, many from Scotland, were hired to take landscapes and artfully create their visions for the new courses. Many of the top hundred private — and public — golf courses in North America are the product of their work. Golf course architecture evolved from a hobby to a viable and lucrative occupation.

Many of the golden age designers spent time in England and Scotland studying the courses there, using what they learned when sketching their plans for the new courses across North America. The greatest Canadian designer, Stanley Thompson (who co-founded the American Society of Golf Course Architects in 1948), is credited for designing more than 120 golf courses in his lifetime.

RAGS TO RICHES TALE OF IGGY KANEFF

Born in a small agricultural village in north eastern Bulgaria, Ignat Kaneff was one of seven children. At fourteen, he was sent to Austria to work in a vegetable garden to support his family. When Ignat, who became known as "Iggy," immigrated to Canada from Bulgaria in 1951, he had $5 to his name and slept in a garage for the first four months.

He supported himself by taking odd jobs — washing cars, dishes, and floors — before landing a job as a labourer for a building company. He wasn't content to remain someone's employee, however, and in 1956 he founded Kaneff Construction. He eventually grew this into a billion-dollar real estate development business.

After giving golf a try one day and making par on his first hole, Kaneff decided to add building golf courses to his growing investment portfolio; it was also a way for him to offer more golf choices to the Ontario public in the Greater Toronto Area. His first course, built in the 1990s, was Lionhead Golf Club and Conference Centre. The club hosted a skins game featuring Arnold Palmer not long after it opened.

Under the umbrella Kaneff Golf, over the years he built five additional courses: Royal Ontario Golf Club, Carlisle Golf & Country Club, Streetsville Glen Golf Club, and Century Pines Golf Club. When he died on July 12, 2020, at the age of ninety-three, the billionaire philanthropist left a legacy in his adopted country that golfers continue to play and enjoy.

A STEP BACK IN TIME

First built in 1884, near White Sulphur Springs, West Virginia, Oakhurst Links is the first course constructed in the United States, predating by a few years the St. Andrews Golf Club in Yonkers, New York. This links-style course was a nod to the original Scottish courses when it opened and still is today.

The nine-hole course was laid out in 1884 on the estate of Russell Montague. The first recorded tournament on American soil happened at Oakhurst in 1888. Gradually, the course fell into disuse and closed in 1912. Lewis Keller purchased the property in 1959 as a summer retreat to raise his horses and finally, in 1994, decided to recreate and revive these historic nine holes for a new generation. On this links course, where sheep roamed the fairways, golfers were required to use replica hickory clubs, hit gutta percha golf balls, and form tees from a mound of sand — just like the Scots did in the early days of the nineteenth century.

In 2012 the nearby Greenbrier Resort purchased the course. Unfortunately, there was a flood in the area in 2016, when over twenty-four hours, 211 millimetres of rain fell on White Sulphur Springs — making it one of the deadliest in West Virginia history and causing the indefinite closure of Oakhurst Links. Whether it ever reopens or not, this historic course remains an important piece of golf history in North America and is listed on the National Register of Historic Places.

NO MONKEYING AROUND

Built on a former sugar plantation, Sandy Lane Resort in St. James, Barbados, dates back to the 1930s. A getaway for royalty and celebrities alike, past guests include American poet T.S. Eliot, British musician Elton John, opera singer Maria Callas, and Queen Elizabeth II. Rihanna, the second-best-selling female artist of all time, who was born on the Caribbean island, owns a beachside home adjacent to the posh property at 1 Sandy Lane.

In 1998 a trio of wealthy Irish businessmen purchased the property: J.P. McManus, Dermot Desmond, and John Magnier. These investors promptly razed the resort and initiated a three-year, $450 million renovation that included reimagining the property's original nine-hole course and designing two new championship eighteen-hole layouts.

The Green Monkey is one of three golf courses at the luxurious resort; there is also the eighteen-hole Country Club and the nine-hole Old Nine.

When it opened in 2000, the Green Monkey (named in homage to the Bajan primates, first brought to Barbados by European explorers in the seventeenth century, that roam the island) was reported to be the most expensive course ever built — the price tag was $25 million. American golf course architect Tom Fazio used this big budget to design a masterpiece that incorporates natural features like the coral walls that tower over the fairways into a 7,343-yard championship layout. It's definitely not your typical resort course. The signature hole is the par 3 sixteenth, which plays more than two hundred yards downhill and features a whimsically shaped bunker with a manicured grass monkey in the front of the trap.

The Green Monkey is available for play by hotel guests only. The green fees are $400, but it's important to keep in mind that the cheapest room at this swanky resort costs $1,000.

THE INVISIBLE WINNER

Golf's popularity surged in the 1960s, due in part to the fame of the larger-than-life PGA Tour stars, collectively called the Big Three (Jack Nicklaus, Arnold Palmer, and Gary Player), who TV helped make household names, even for non-golf fans. All three had personalities as colourful as their games. The media heaped lots of attention on these three, while other excellent golfers never really got their time in the spotlight. One of these was Billy Casper.

The story goes that a Tour veteran told Casper when he turned pro in 1955 that he would be better off getting a "nice job selling insurance." The quiet Casper made him eat those words. With fifty-one wins (including three majors: two U.S. Opens and one Masters), he is ranked seventh on the all-time PGA winners list. That is just one less victory than Byron Nelson and more wins than many other more well-known players, like Tom Watson, Walter Hagen, and Gene Sarazen, collected in their careers. From 1968 to 1970, Casper won thirteen tournaments — the Big Three only managed sixteen combined. He was the Tour's player of the year twice and also added five Vardon Trophies for the lowest scoring average. In a co-written foreword to his memoir, *The Big Three and Me*, published in 2012, those three golf titans stated, "It could have been the Big Four," and in his own autobiography, Nicklaus reiterated this fact, writing, "The trio should really have been a quartet."

Why wasn't Casper as well-known and loved as Nicklaus, Palmer, and Player? For one thing, he didn't have the swagger, good looks, and on-course personality of the Big Three he competed against. Casper's game was consistent, conservative, and methodical. This style of play certainly played a role in the fact that his accomplishments were always overshadowed and he did not get the due he rightly deserved.

Unfortunately, the media often focused on Casper's off-course exploits and personal life (like his conversion to Mormonism in 1966 and his diet of buffalo meat and organically grown vegetables).

While acknowledged by those who competed against him, the media underrated him during his playing days. Hopefully, this piece will help to shine a little light on Billy Casper — one of golf's greatest unknown players.

ACKNOWLEDGEMENTS

A book like this does not happen without a team. First, thanks to the amazing, ongoing support from the folks at Dundurn Press. Flashback more than seven years. This publisher took a chance on this wannabe author who had yet to pen a book. Four books later I am forever grateful. Special shout-outs go to Kathryn Lane, Kwame Scott Fraser, Chris Houston, and Elena Radic.

I've learned throughout my career that every writer needs an even better editor. For this book, I was lucky to have my father, who proofed and provided feedback on early drafts of many of the stories you just read. Thanks, Dad! Once I finished my final draft and submitted it to Dundurn, I was paired with Dominic Farrell. Over the course of several months, Dominic worked with me to fine-tune the text, improve the flow, and ask those questions the reader might have had if I had not provided more detail. It was a pleasure working with Dominic; he brought a professionalism, flair, and attention to detail to the finished book.

As I mentioned in the introduction, I owe a lot of gratitude when it comes to my golf-writing career to Lorne Rubenstein. Anyone who has followed golf in Canada over the past forty plus years knows Lorne's byline. I'm fortunate to call Lorne a colleague and a friend. Thanks for meeting me for a coffee at Bayview Village all those years ago, Rube. You are a mentor and I'm forever grateful for your support of my writing and for sharing your passion of this great game with me over the past twenty-five years. My apologies for exposing you to my chipping yips and my sometimes erratic golf shots.

A nod as well goes to all of the golf editors I've worked with writing about the game, who always made my final published words sound better — especially Helen Ross and Mike McAllister (PGATOUR.com); Alison King and John Tenpenny (*Golf Canada*); Scott Hollister (*Golf Course Management*); Mike Zawacki and Guy Cipriano (*Golf Course Industry*); Ted McIntyre (*Ontario Golf*); and John Gordon and Tim O'Connor (*ClubLink Life*).

Thanks to Meggan Gardner, director, Heritage Services at Golf Canada, who opened up the extensive library at the

Canadian Golf Hall of Fame, where I spent many days researching stories for this book. And a special nod as well to all of my fellow golf writing colleagues and Golf Journalist of Canada Association board members, who continue to seek out — and to share — fascinating stories, like the ones in this book.

Finally, to my family: my incredible wife, Patricia, and my two adult children, Alex and Isabella. There are never enough words to express my love and gratitude for your support of my writing life and my everyday weirdness. Thanks for keeping me focused and for always being my biggest cheerleaders. *Abrazos.*

ABOUT THE AUTHOR

David McPherson is the best-selling author of *101 Fascinating Canadian Music Facts*, *Massey Hall*, and *The Legendary Horseshoe Tavern: A Complete History*. His love of golf began at age eleven, when his father gifted his family the best Christmas present ever: a membership to Westmount Golf & Country Club. Past president of the Golf Journalists Association of Canada and a Golf Writers Association of America member, over the past twenty-five years, David's work has appeared in PGATOUR.com, SCOREGolf, *Golf Digest*, *Golf Canada*, *Golf Course Architecture*, *Golf Course Management*, and *Golf Course Industry*. He lives in Waterloo, Ontario.